THE REIGN OF
THE REPTILES

THE REIGN OF
THE REPTILES

Dr. Michael J. Benton

Eagle
Editions

A QUANTUM BOOK

Published by Eagle Editions
an imprint of Eagle Remainders Ltd
2A Kingsway, Royston
Hertfordshire SG8 5EG

Copyright ©1990 Quarto Publishing Ltd

This edition printed 1998

ISBN 1-902328-17-5

QUMPRD

This book is produced by
Quantum Books Ltd
6 Blundell Street
London N7 9BH

Printed in Singapore by
Star Standard Industries Pte Ltd

CONTENTS

INTRODUCTION

Reptiles of today - animals such as turtles, crocodiles, lizards and snakes - may not seem very impressive or diverse. Yet in the past, their ancestors ruled the Earth. Their reign lasted some 235 million years, much longer than the 65 million years of dominance enjoyed by the mammals, the group to which humans belong.

Ancient 'sea monsters' from a popular science book dated about 1880, showing an imaginary battle set against a thunderous backdrop!

The reign of the reptiles followed millions of years of the evolution of vertebrates (animals with backbones), which in turn followed an even longer period when complex forms of life evolved from simple beginnings. This part of the story, the appearance and early history of life, is told first, in order to provide a firm foundation

Ancient "sea monsters" from a popular science book dated about 1880, showing an imaginary battle set against a thunderous backdrop!

for the detailed descriptions of key steps in reptilian evolution in later chapters.

The reign of the reptiles falls into several distinct phases: the early years, during the Carboniferous period; the dominance of the mammal-like reptiles during the Permian and Triassic periods; and the rise of the dinosaurs, the flying pterosaurs marine ichthyosaurs, plesiosaurs and others during the Triassic, Jurassic and Cretaceous periods. The end of the reptiles came 65 million years ago, during the famous extinction events that wiped out the dinosaurs and many other reptiles and other groups of animals.

THE FIRST REPTILE FOSSILS

How can we know about these events of so long ago? Fossils are our keys to the past. The first fossil reptiles were collected in the seventeenth century, when scientists recorded peculiar large bones from various parts of Europe. However, these were poorly understood at the time, since geologists had very rudimentary ideas about the history of the Earth and the history of life. Indeed, many held to a literal biblical interpretation of events and were therefore unable to allow a great age for the Earth, nor to conceive of the idea of extinction. To admit that species of plants or animals had existed in the distant past, but no longer exist today, would have been tantamount to criticising the Creator for producing an organism that was not viable.

During the eighteenth century, numerous remains of reptiles were recorded, and many were almost complete fossilized skeletons. For example, a splendid skeleton of a marine crocodilian was excavated from the shore at

Whitby, in north-eastern England, in 1754. Reported as a 'fossile allegator' in the *Philosophical Transactions of the Royal Society*, of London, the author entered into complex arguments to prove that the animal was truly found within the rock at the foot of a high cliff. The bones were enough like a modern crocodilian to cause little surprise, but the discoverer had to make a strong case that this was an ancient fossil, buried beneath thick layers of mudstone and limestone, and not a recently deceased curiosity.

Other discoveries of the time were harder to interpret, since they were bones of animals that bore no relation to modern forms. In 1776, the remains of a giant skull were excavated from the well-known chalk quarries of the Maastricht area in Holland by a German army surgeon, Dr. Hoffmann. He was collecting fossils for the Haarlem Museum and returned there with his spectacular find. The skull was nearly complete, its jaws armed with large, sharp teeth. Its size indicated an animal up to 33 feet (10 meters) long. Understandably, the specimen caused a sensation. The noted Dutch anatomy expert, Peter Camper, interpreted the monster as an archaic whale, and his scientific description circulated throughout Europe. At this point, the owner of the quarries, Canon Godin, realised that he had let a very valuable specimen slip past, and he sued in the courts for its return. Having recovered the skull, he locked it up and would not show it to anyone. This was especially frustrating because of the renown of the find, and because it

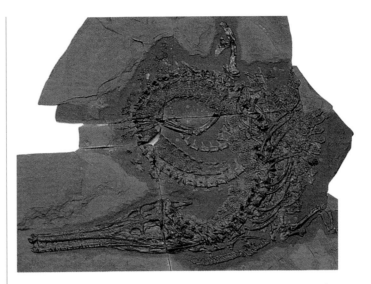

The rolled-up skeleton of a marine crocodilian, Steneosaurus, from the Lower Jurassic of Germany. It is similar to the "fossile allegators" reported in the mid-18th century.

seemed to be the first conclusive proof of a giant extinct reptile.

A second discovery at about this time also hinted at the great diversity of extinct reptiles in former times. In 1784, Cosmo Alessandro Collini, an Italian writer and naturalist, published an illustrated description of "an unknown amphibious marine animal of dubious zoological classification" which he had discovered earlier in a limestone quarry at Solnhofen, southern Germany. The fossil specimen was a complete skeleton of a small animal with a long pointed beak, large eyes, short legs,

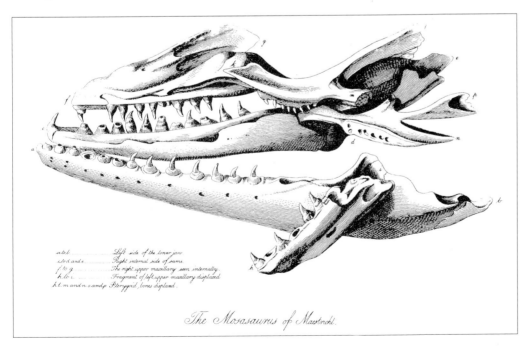

a to b.   Left side of the lower jaw.
c to d and e   Right internal side of same.
f to g   The right upper maxillary seen internally.
h to i   Fragment of left upper maxillary displaced
k. l. m and n. o and p. Pterygoid, bones displaced.

The Mosasaurus of Maestricht.

The Mosasaurus of Maastricht, the celebrated partial skull of a Late Cretaceous giant sea-going lizard that was found in chalk quarries in Holland. The remains consist of the two halves of the lower jaw, parts of the skull, and a part of the snout displaced to the bottom right. This illustration is from the English edition of Georges Cuvier's The Animal Kingdom (1830).

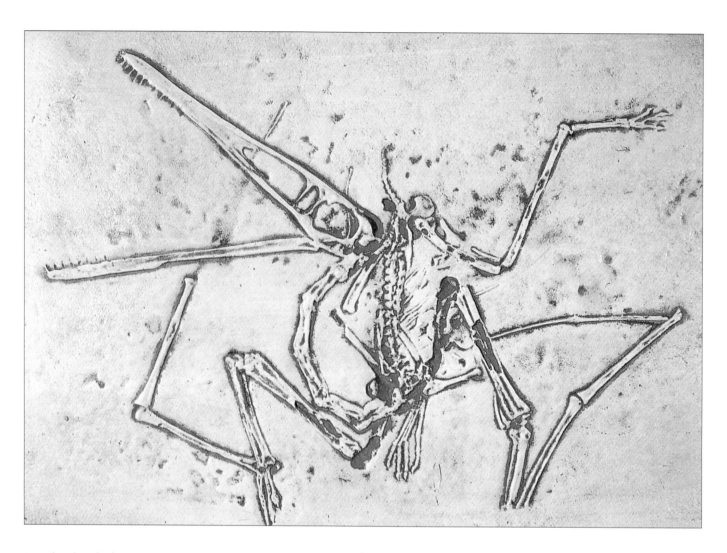

Pterodactylus, the first pterosaur to be found. The head is almost all jaw, and the body bends up behind. One leg stretches up to the top right, and the long fingers supporting the wing are bent over on each side.

and extremely long, thin arms. Like the Maastricht monster, it became the subject of much controversy. One German professor suggested that the bones were those of a water bird, while another argued that it must have swum in the oceans, using its elongated arms like giant paddles. Yet other scientists of the day said that it was a bat or an "epicene creature, half bird and half bat." *Pterodactylus*, the first pterosaur to be found. The head is almost all jaw, and the body bends up behind. One leg stretches up to the top right, and the long fingers supporting the wing are bent over on each side.

CUVIER'S CONTRIBUTIONS

The true identity of both of these strange fossil specimens was established by Baron Georges Cuvier (1769-

1832), the celebrated French anatomist. He moved to Paris in 1795 and held various high positions there, both at the new Natural History Museum, and also in office under the revolutionary, Napoleonic, and later administrations. In 1795, French troops were positioned outside Maastricht. Cuvier arranged for the large skull to be saved when the soldiers stormed the town. They entered Maastricht and carefully left Canon Godin's house unscathed. However, the churchman feared for the safety of his fossil, and at the dead of night he had it moved to a hiding place elsewhere in the city. The French general heard of this, and he offered 600 bottles of wine to the second discoverer of the skull. Needless to say, the soldiers ransacked the town. Next morning, twelve grenadiers reported to the general with the monstrous fossil and collected their reward.

The skull was sent to Paris, where Cuvier recognised it at once as that of a giant varanid lizard. (It was later named *Mosasaurus hoffmanni* by the British palaeontologist Conybeare, in honour of its first discoverer.) Cuvier shunned convoluted arguments, discussions of mythical and biblical monsters, or appeals to the hidden wonders yet to be dredged from the depths of the oceans, in making this identification. He used the techniques of strict comparative anatomy - that is, a comparison of the shapes of the bones, and their relations to each other, with the bones of known animals. He could tell that *Mosasaurus* was a reptile, because of the nature of its teeth and the shape of its bones. It was clearly a lizard, because it shared all the specialized features of the skull roof seen in modern lizards. It was a varanid lizard, because of the shape of the jaws and skull bones. No matter that modern varanid lizards - the monitor lizards of southern continents - never reach more than seven feet (two meters) in length, and live on land. Mosasaurus was anatomically the same, only much bigger.

Cuvier also resolved the identity of Collini's bird/bat/swimming reptile, an even trickier problem since it had no obvious living relatives. In 1801, working only from the excellent illustration of it in Collini's paper, Cuvier again applied his rigorous knowledge of comparative anatomy. The animal was obviously a reptile, not a bird or a bat, and it was obviously a flyer because it had wings, and not paddles for swimming. The very long arm was made up mainly from an elongated fourth finger, which must have borne a membrane of skin in life. Cuvier named the pterodactyle, meaning

A large plant-eating dinosaur, Shunosaurus from the Middle Jurassic of China (above). The first dinosaurs were named in the 1820s, and at the time they were as mysterious as the other fossil reptiles.

"wing-finger," an actively flying reptile that probably fed on insects.

THE FINDS OF MARY ANNING

Further finds of abundant marine reptiles were made in southern England during the early years of the nineteenth century. Mary Anning (1799-1847) was the first professional fossil collector on record. She helped her father in his souvenir shop in the English resort of Lyme Regis, by collecting fossils from the local shorelines for sale to tourists. In 1811, she came upon some giant bones lying in the grey mudstones at the foot of the cliff. Recognising their potential value, she dug them out over several weeks in 1811-12, and agreed to sell them to Sir Everard Home, professor of anatomy and surgery at

A delightful view of the Mesozoic world presented in a popular science book of 1881. The reptiles look distinctly dragon-like, and they are all apparently intent on eating each other!

The ichthyosaur Stenopterygius quadriscissus (above) from the Lower Jurassic of Holzmaden, near Stuttgart, southern Germany. This locality has long been famous for the exquisite preservation of marine reptiles, fishes, and other fossils. All the bones of the skeleton, including the long-snouted skull, the paddles, and the backbone, are preserved. There are even indications of the skin's outline, showing a dorsal fin on the back.

London University, who happened to be visiting Lyme Regis at the time. Home pondered the identity of his purchase: was it a fish, amphibian, reptile, or whale? He wrote an illustrated description of the animal in 1814 and interpreted it as a fish. More specimens came to light soon after, and in 1818, he wrote a second paper in which he argued that the animal had similarities to the living duck-billed platypus, a primitive mammal of Australia. Finally, in 1819, he decided that the bones came from an amphibian, because of their curious mixture of fish-like aquatic features and reptilian terrestrial characters. This remarkable catalogue of confusions was brought to an end in the 1820s, when many new specimens were reported. Several English palaeontologists, as well as Cuvier, argued that the animal - now named *Ichthyosaurus* ('fish-reptile') - was an entirely extinct form of marine reptile.

Mary Anning also found the first well-preserved skeleton of another major group of extinct marine reptiles, the plesiosaurs. Odd bones had been found at various times, but in 1824 she uncovered a nearly complete specimen, named *Plesiosaurus* ("near-reptile"), which had a long neck, small head, and large paddles for limbs. Also about this time, the first two dinosaurs were named: the carnivore *Megalosaurus* in 1824, and the herbivore *Iguanodon* in 1825, based on fossilized bones found in England, near Oxford and in Sussex respectively. Thus, by 1830, five major groups of extinct reptiles were known: dinosaurs, ichthyosaurs, plesiosaurs, mosasaurs, and pterosaurs.

Further discoveries were made throughout Europe in the years following 1830. Most importantly, specimens were coming to light in other continents, too. Vast collections of the bones of all of these reptile groups were made in North America in the second half of the nineteenth century, as well as more primitive reptiles from the Permian and Triassic rocks of Texas and Arizona. Further important discoveries were also made in southern Africa, a major source of Permian and Triassic mammal-like reptiles. This century, increased collecting efforts worldwide by hundreds of palaeontologists, spurred on by the desire to expand our knowledge and also by public interest, have turned up hundreds of species of fossil reptiles in all continents. New finds con-

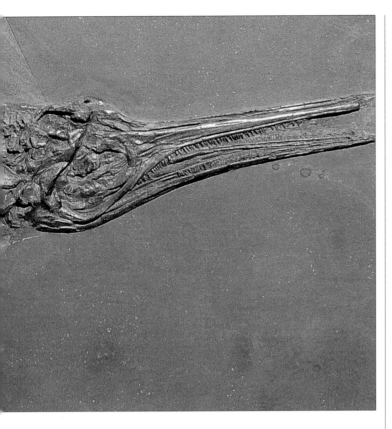

The limb bones of a large herbivorous dinosaur in the process of excavation (top right). Skeletons of the giant reptiles of the past are often preserved nearly complete in the rocks, but the sedimentary processes that acted before burial - for example, being moved by river currents - may break them up and scatter the bones. But the fossils give enough information for full-scale restorations of the skeleton, the external appearance, and even the lifestyle of the original animal.

tinue to be made every day.

THE SIGNIFICANCE OF THE REPTILES' REIGN

This book tells the story of the history and diversity of fossil reptiles, many of which are quite bizarre and unlike any living animal. It is an important story because of the reptiles' long tenure as dominant animals on land, and at times in the sea and air. In addition, it is important because both birds and mammals originated from these extinct reptile groups. The dinosaurs are probably the best-known fossil reptiles, but many of the groups described in this book were just as significant in the fascinating and ever-changing scenes played out during the history of the Earth.

Michael Benton

Michael J. Benton
Bristol, January 1990

THE EVOLUTION OF REPTILES AND THEIR RELATIVES

The evolutionary tree shown is the closest approximation that palaeontologists can give at present to the true pattern of the evolution of the major reptile groups and their ancestors, the amphibians and the fishes. It has two axes that both convey a great deal of information: the horizontal time axis, and the vertical divergence axis.

The time axis gives the names of the stratigraphic periods during which the reptiles existed, as well as exact ages, in millions of years before the present. The stratigraphic periods are global standards set up by field geologists last century. They are based on the changing characteristics of the rocks, and the fossils they contain, through time. The exact ages are based on radiometric dating of selected rocks, and this work is still in progress. Certain rocks contain unstable, or naturally radioactive, minerals that change their composition in a regular way; the patterns of change allow exact dates to be calculated.

The divergence axis gives a general indication of the degree of relatedness of the groups. The branching pattern of the evolutionary tree is based on recent cladistic analyses of the characters of fossil and living reptiles. The shading indicates the known fossil distribution.

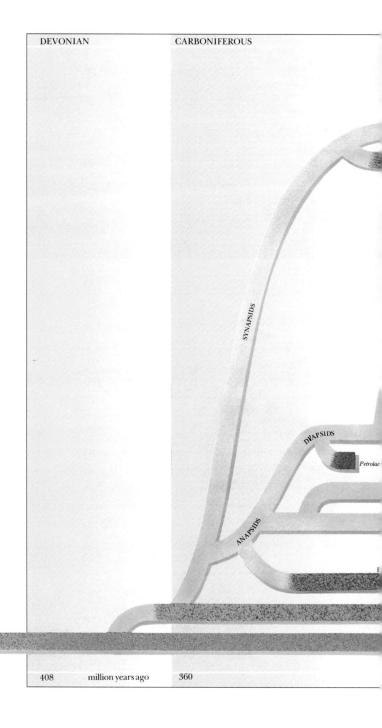

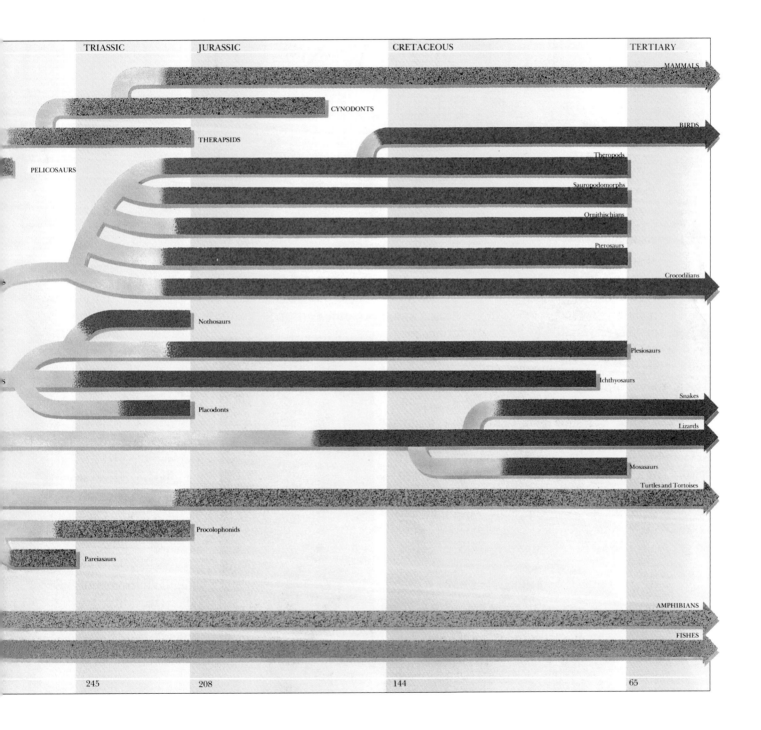

TRIASSIC JURASSIC CRETACEOUS TERTIARY

MAMMALS

CYNODONTS

THERAPSIDS

BIRDS

PELICOSAURS

Theropods

Sauropodomorphs

Ornithischians

Pterosaurs

Crocodilians

Nothosaurs

Plesiosaurs

Ichthyosaurs

Snakes

Placodonts

Lizards

Mosasaurs

Turtles and Tortoises

Procolophonids

Pareiasaurs

AMPHIBIANS

FISHES

245 208 144 65

CHAPTER

THE DAWN OF AN ERA

The beginning of the reign of the reptiles can be dated at about 300 million years ago, during the Late Carboniferous period. It lasted until the famous mass extinctions at the end of the Cretaceous period, 65 million years ago. Reptiles came on the scene relatively late in the day, since the Earth was formed perhaps 4,500 million years ago, and the first forms of life date from about 3,500 million years ago.

The fossil record of the early stages in the evolution of life is generally poor, with only a few remarkable glimpses of what was happening during those distant millennia. Rare but spectacular fossils show that the first vertebrates (animals with backbones) arose 510 million years ago; that fishes evolved dramatically thereafter and gave rise to the first land vertebrates, the amphibians, 365 million years ago; and the amphibians in turn led to the first reptiles, 25 million years later, who gradually spread to take over the world.

THE ORIGIN OF THE UNIVERSE

The Universe is said to have come into existence 13,500 million years ago, in a sequence of spectacular but unimaginable events called the Big Bang - which lasted for a total of about one second! Dates for the age of the Universe are of course highly conjectural, and estimates range from less than 8,000 million to over 20,000 million years. Equally, the Big Bang theory and the

sequence of events that it includes are also conjectural, being based on studies of particle physics, cosmology, and advanced mathematics.

Before the Big Bang, time and space did not exist as separate entities. They were combined so intimately as to be unrecognisable, into a state scientists call space-time. The Big Bang theory itself hinges on the idea of inflation. A very small volume of space-time expanded a little and cooled. Then a cosmological force, acting like repulsive gravity, inflated the Universe very rapidly. The expansion continues today at more-measurable rates, as the galaxies recede from each other and from our own galaxy, the Milky Way.

The first small expansion of the Universe, to roughly the size of a tennis ball, took 10^{-43} seconds - that is, ten million million million million million million millionths of a second. The

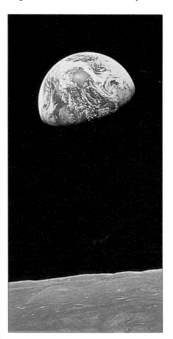

What makes the Earth different from its sister planets is its possession of an atmosphere that contains the key gases essential for the evolution of life.

The swirling clouds of the Trifid Nebula contain enough gas to make
many stars like our Sun, which was born 4,550 million years ago.
Following this event, the planets of the Solar System evolved.

major expansion of the Universe began almost immediately, at 10^{-38} seconds after its origin, and the immense energy contained in the original space-time entity was directed outward, in the form of matter and radiation.

When the Universe was about three minutes old, there was an enormous thermonuclear explosion that created the nuclei (central parts) of atoms of the gas helium. But the first complete atoms did not form until about 300,000 years later, as a result of immense pressure waves. It then took several thousand million years for the clouds of helium gas to separate and form galaxies. The gas made the galaxies luminous by condensing into stars. It was not until some 10,000 million years ago that our galaxy, the Milky Way, was formed. Then, following a great explosion and rapid shrinkage of gas clouds, our Sun was formed 4,550 million years ago. The familiar planets of our Solar System, including the Earth, were created from a flattened cloud of gas, ice,

The Scottish Old Red Sandstone fish Cheiracanthus, *a spiny acanthodian. This example shows a typical mode of preservation, in which the small fish is enclosed in a nodule, which the collector has split open.*

and radioactive dust swirling around the newborn Sun. These constituents collided and coagulated to form the nuclei of the planets, which attracted additional material under the force of gravity. It took 100 million years for all the materials of the Earth to be assembled. At this stage, the Earth probably attracted its Moon, possibly itself an embryonic planet, into its orbit, to be held there by the force of its gravity.

THE EARLY EARTH AND THE ORIGIN OF LIFE

The early Earth was extremely hot and rent by volcanic eruptions. They belched out clouds of steam and debris which fell onto a surface that was gradually cooling. When the temperature fell below 212°F (100°C), water began to collect in depressions, to form the first oceans. These seas and pools were filled with a strange cocktail of chemicals, often called the "primeval soup," which included carbon dioxide, nitrogen, and methane, but no "free" oxygen (or oxygen un-combined with other matter).

These simple chemicals readily combined to form more complex compounds such as amino acids and polysaccharides, the building blocks of living matter. Experiments with reconstituted "primeval soup" in the laboratory have shown how these more complex compounds form under the influence of electrical discharges - the scientist's analogies for the violent lightning and electrical storms that must have beset the early Earth. After experimental heating, again a likely laboratory analogy for the effects of volcanic eruptions in the primeval world, the amino acids linked to produce polypeptides. These are the subunits of proteins, essential components of living things. Some of the characteristics of life have been mimicked in laboratories where polypeptide soups can be induced to form cell-like structures with membranes, which reproduce themselves after a fashion. As yet, life itself has not been created in the laboratory; but the above-described experiments show how the essential steps may have occurred.

It is likely that life arose about 3,900 million years ago, but the oldest convincing fossil evidence dates from 400 million years later. The fossils do not look much like living things at first, more like inorganic (non-living), layered boulders. However, these structures, called stromatolites, still exist and live today. They consist of interleaved mats of blue-green algae and muddy sediments.

Blue-green algae are very primitive single-celled organisms that lack a nucleus (prokaryotes) and have other simple characteristics; in this respect, they resemble bacteria. They form flat, thin 'mats' in shallow, warm waters where they photosynthesise - that is, convert the energy of sunlight, in combination with water and gaseous carbon dioxide, into living tissue. This process requires the green protein substance chlorophyll, hence the green color of the blue-green algae (and most other plants). In time, the algal mat is covered by a layer of sediment which masks the sun. The mat responds by sending filaments upward to re-form itself on the sunlit surface of the sediment. Over many years, the cycle is repeated, and a multi-layered, cabbage-like structure is produced. This is the stromatolite. Even if the organic remnants of the blue-green algae are lost in the fossils, the internal structure of a stromatolite is a sure key to its living origins.

Actual fossils of blue-green algae and bacteria have been tentatively identified from Australian rocks similar in age to the oldest stromatolites. All that can be seen are narrow filaments consisting of several compartments, just like the strings of cells formed by some modern blue-green algae. More comprehensive remains of bacteria and blue-green algae have been found in the 3,000-million-year-old Fig Tree Chert rocks of South Africa. They include filaments, as well as spheres that appear to show various stages of cell division. More complex prokaryotes have been found in rocks 1,900 million years old, the Gunflint Chert of Canada. They include some that look like stars.

COMPLEX CELLS AND MULTICELLS

Except for blue-green algae and bacteria, which are prokaryotes (lacking a nucleus), all other living plants and animals are termed eukaryotes. Each of their cells has a nucleus which contains chromosomes, the controlling chemicals that carry the genetic code instructions

Middle Cambrian stromatolites from Hubei, China. These large, layered, pillar-like structures have proved to be abundant in certain ancient rocks, and they include the earliest representations of life. The layered structure in each pillar has been built up by organic action.

for building the whole organism. There are also structures called organelles inside the cells, but outside the nucleus.

It is widely believed that the organelles - such as energy-producing mitochondria in plants and animals, and the photosynthesising chloroplasts in plants - arose by a process termed symbiosis. This is the close and mutual cooperation of two or more organisms. The idea is that a large ameba-like prokaryote engulfed smaller prokaryotes that could photosynthesise or produce energy. In their turn, the consumed prokaryotes gained protection and nutrition from their larger host, and so became permanent parts of the cellular machinery.

The most primitive living eukaryotes are algae and protozoans (single-celled animals). They arose at least 1,400 million years ago, and their spherical or many-pointed fossils are interpreted as such because they are far larger than typical prokaryotes - up to one millimetre in diameter, compared to less than 20 micrometers (0.02 millimetres) for prokaryotes. The oldest protozoans, dated at 800 million years old, had rigid vase-shaped skeletons which improved their chances of fossilization.

continued on page 20

THE GEOLOGICAL TIME SCALE

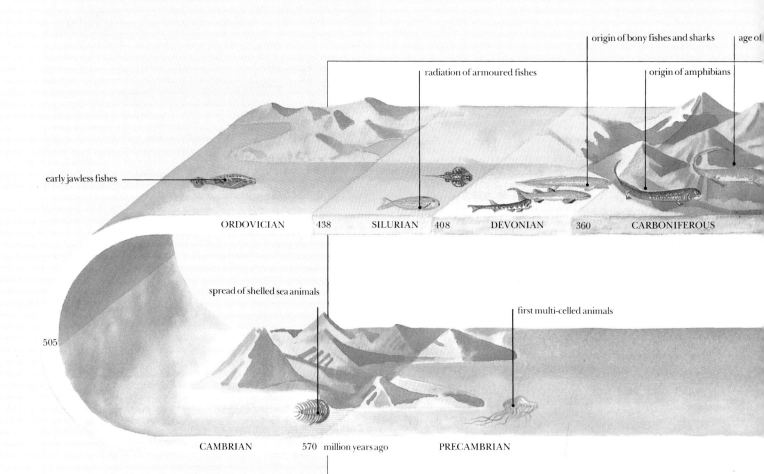

origin of bony fishes and sharks | age of

radiation of armoured fishes

origin of amphibians

early jawless fishes

ORDOVICIAN — 438 — SILURIAN — 408 — DEVONIAN — 360 — CARBONIFEROUS

spread of shelled sea animals

first multi-celled animals

505

CAMBRIAN — 570 — million years ago — PRECAMBRIAN

The ribbon diagram is an attempt to represent the pattern of the history of the Earth, and of the history of life, as established by geologists and paleontologists. It is very hard to comprehend the magnitude of geological time – all 4,600 million years of it – and it is very hard to realise that the well-known parts of evolution, such as the dinosaurs or early humans, fit into only a tiny segment of the entire history of the Earth.

The time scale shows two aspects. First, the *sequence* of events, or *relative* dating, has been determined by examining the record of the rocks. In general, older fossils occur in older rocks lower down in the pile. The second aspect, the *absolute* dates, are based on more recent work using radioactive isotopes in the rocks: dates can be determined by studying the amount of natural radioactive decay.

The first 4,000 million years of the history of the Earth (right), generally termed the Precambrian, seems to have witnessed relatively little in the way of major geological or evolutionary advances. However, this is a serious misconception based on our lack of knowledge of those ancient times, and the fact that many of the advances in the history of life that occurred then seem minor.

The Earth arose some 4,600 million years ago, condensing from scattered matter in the Milky Way. For the first 1,000 million years or so, the surface of the Earth was uninhabitable: it was composed of

molten rock, and volcanoes erupted frequently. There was no air or water. The surface of the Earth cooled (1), and water may have condensed from volcanic vapours 4,000 million years ago (2). The oldest rocks are dated from just after that (3). Conditions had become stable enough at last for life to survive.

The first evidence of life, appeared about 3,500 million years ago (4): stromatolites formed by blue-green algae. The Earth continued to be affected by major volcanic episodes (5). The early living microscopic creatures began to produce oxygen (6), and the first

true plants appeared after that (7). This was followed, towards the end of the Precambrian, by the appearance of multi-celled animals (8), and then the radiation of animals with shells, some 570 million years ago (9), the beginning of the well-known fossil record.

The time scale is expanded (above) to show all the events that took place during the last 570 million years, even though this is only one-ninth of the age of the Earth.

The ribbon diagram is an attempt to represent the pattern of the history of the Earth, and of the history of life, as established by geologists and palaeontologists. It is very hard to comprehend the magnitude of geological time - all 4,600 million years of it - and it is very hard to realise that the well-known parts of evolution, such as the dinosaurs or early humans, fit into only a tiny segment of the entire history of the Earth.

The time scale shows two aspects. First, the sequence of events, or relative dating, has been determined by examining the record of the rocks. In general, older fossils occur in older rocks lower down in the pile. The second aspect, the absolute dates, are based on more recent work using radioactive isotopes in the rocks: dates can be determined by studying the amount of natural radioactive decay.

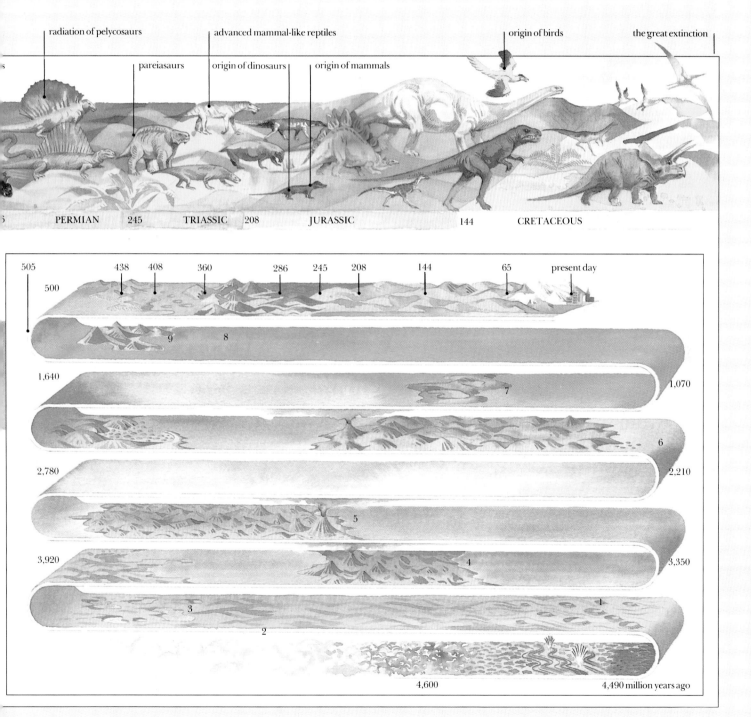

radiation of pelycosaurs | advanced mammal-like reptiles | origin of birds | the great extinction

pareiasaurs | origin of dinosaurs | origin of mammals

PERMIAN 245 TRIASSIC 208 JURASSIC 144 CRETACEOUS

505 438 408 360 286 245 208 144 65 present day
500
9 8
1,640 1,070
7
6
2,780 2,210
5
3,920 3,350
4
3
2 1
4,600 4,490 million years ago

The next important step from these various single-celled life forms was the evolution of multi-celled organisms. Although the blue-green algae could form filaments and mats, the cells did not really live together and cooperate in an intimate way. A truly multi-celled organism always has more than one cell, and generally many thousands or millions; and these cells are closely interconnected and interdependent. The possession of many cells allowed organisms to become larger, and it encouraged the cells to become specialised so that some concentrated on feeding, others on reproduction, and others on defense. The oldest multicelled fossils are possibly seaweeds from North America, dated at 1,300-800 million years ago. Further evidence consists of poorly dated "trace" fossils - burrows and tracks and trails, rather than the creatures themselves - in Norwegian sandstones, that indicate the presence of complex animals with limbs or other means of locomotion.

EDIACARA: A GLIMPSE OF EARLY COMPLEX LIFE

Our first glimpse of the diversity of multicelled animal life comes from isolated, but spectacular, fossils from several parts of the world.

During the 1940s, some remarkably well-preserved fossils of jellyfish were found in the Ediacara Hills in South Australia, in rocks about 680 million years old. Subsequently, fossils of sea creatures such as sea pens, worms, arthropods (crab-like animals), and some truly bizarre forms, turned up in the Ediacara Hills - nearly all soft-bodied animals. Experts realised that they closely resembled animals already found in Sweden, England, and Africa. It is clear now that the so-called "Ediacara fauna" had a nearly worldwide distribution.

The most remarkable thing about these animals is that they would not normally be preserved as fossils. Jellyfish, sea pens, and worms have no hard skeletons of

A soft-bodied animal resembling a sea pen, from an Ediacara-type fauna in Newfoundland, Canada. The sea pens are coelenterates (the group including jellyfish and corals). The creature's attachment disk lies to the left, and the feather-shaped filtering device to the right.

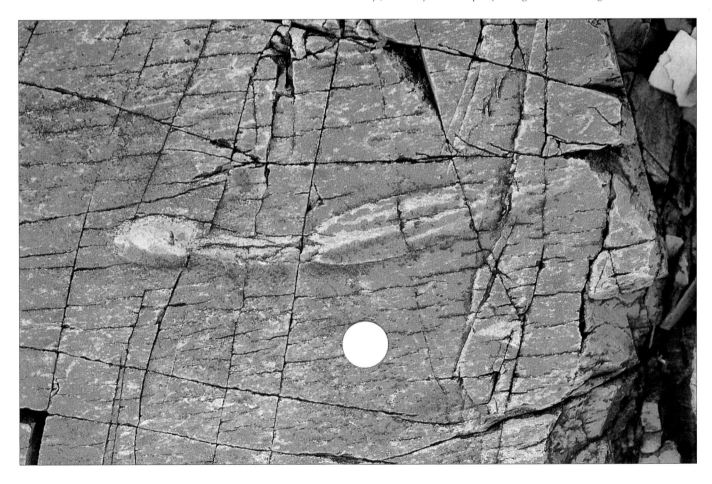

the type that can readily form a fossil. Normally, after death, the flesh of soft-bodied animals rots away completely, and there is nothing left to be buried. Nonetheless, the Ediacara creatures give us an impression of what life was like 680 million years ago. A moderately diverse assemblage of animals moved about on the sea floor and in the shallow waters above, and some were attached to the bottom.

CAMBRIAN LIFE AND THE ORIGIN OF THE VERTEBRATES

The long history of life that has just been recounted, spanning the time interval between the origin of the Earth, 4,600 million years ago, to a time just after the Ediacara faunas, 570 million years ago, is generally termed the Precambrian. The 570 million years since then, known as the Phanerozoic ('abundant life'), have left a much fuller fossil record that has allowed palaeontologists to delve more deeply into the story of life.

The Precambrian/Phanerozoic boundary is marked by a profound biological advance: the origin of hard parts in many groups of animals. These include calcareous (calcium-based) shells in brachiopods, corals, starfish and other echinoderms, and mollusks; chitin (protein-based) skeletons in crab-like arthropods; siliceous (silicon-based) skeletons in sponges, and phosphatic skeletons in vertebrates and others. The reasons for the independent origin of a skeleton in so many separate groups is still a mystery. Explanations range from major changes in ocean chemistry to evolutionary pressures from continually new forms of voracious predators.

A glimpse of these early hard-skeleton animals of the Cambrian period, the first part of the Phanerozoic, may be seen in the famous Burgess Shale fossils of British Columbia, Canada. Since their discovery in 1909, these rock deposits have yielded tens of thousands of fossil specimens of marine animals that belong to over 100 species. The fossils are all exquisitely preserved, showing delicate skeletons, soft tissues, and even gut contents and internal organs. It seems that the animals were living in shallow seas and their carcasses were washed over a steep slope into deep, oxygen-poor water. The lack of oxygen provided perfect conditions for preservation in a fine black mudstone, since there were no scavenging animals and no bacteria to rot away the bodies.

The most remarkable Burgess Shale animals are the arthropods - animals with jointed legs and a thin, chitinous skeleton, which include our modern crabs, spiders, and insects, and their ancestors. Among the Burgess arthropods were trilobites, which had a broad head shield, large eyes, a jointed thorax and tail, and numerous complex legs and gills underneath. Other arthropods were superficially like shrimp, being bizarre and small spiny swimmers, and also giant scorpion-like animals with oar-shaped legs and voracious, grasping mouthparts.

Fixed to the Burgess seabed was a diverse array of sponges, crinoids (sea lilies), and brachiopods (lamp shells). Within the sediment were many worms, including the predatory priapulid worms, whose protrusible hook-bearing proboscis, or mouth tube, was used to seize prey. Some of the worms were broad-bodied swimmers, distantly related to modern lugworms, with delicate arrays of bristles and tufts along the sides of their bodies. Mollusks, some vaguely like limpets with single conical shells, but others with multi-part shells, moved about on the bottom, along with the caterpillar-like onychophores.

The most celebrated Burgess Shale animals are those that do not seem to bear a relation to any other creatures whatsoever. They include *Opabinia*, a long-bodied swimmer with a segmented body, five eyes on stalks, and an appealing flexible trunk at the front which grasped prey with a series of spikes and transferred it to the mouth underneath. The even more amusing *Hallucigenia* moved about on seven pairs of "stilts." It had a head of sorts, a curled tail, and seven flexible

Our earliest ancestor? Pikaia gracilens *from the Middle Cambrian Burgess Shale of British Columbia, Canada. This one and a half inch (40-millimeter) long animal appears to have a slightly enlarged, pointed head to the right, and a slender body divided into numerous, clearly defined muscle blocks, just as in a fish.*

appendages standing upright along the middle of its back.

One of the most important animals from the Burgess Shale is far less spectacular than these strange forms. *Pikaia* looks like a small, squashed sausage, but it may well be the oldest vertebrate, or backboned animal. It has a head, a notochord (the flexible precursor of a backbone), and muscles arranged in V-shaped segments exactly the arrangement seen in modern fishes. In size and shape, Pikaia seems very like today's amphioxus, or lancelet, a very close relative of true fishes.

THE OLDEST FISHES

The first fishes were simple jawless animals like *Pikaia*. It may seem hard to understand how a jawless fish could feed, but certain living fishes, the lampreys and hagfishes, manage very well. They have rings of teeth with which they attach themselves, sucker-like, to the bodies of other fishes, and then they remove lumps of flesh by rasping or twisting.

Many of the early jawless fishes, the first agnathans ("no jaws"), appear to have possessed a substantial amount of body armor. *Arandaspis*, an incompletely known agnathan from the Middle Ordovician (465 million years ago) of Australia, was a bullet-shaped animal with a complex chain-mail of small bony plates covering its head and shoulder region. The armor provided a protective covering against predators such as the giant eurypterids, scorpion-like arthropods that reached lengths of two meters (seven feet) or more and had large claws on their front limbs. *Arandaspis* presumably fed on organic debris and micro-organisms just above the seabed, by sucking them in and ejecting mud and other inedible material.

Fish evolved rapidly in the seas and fresh waters during the subsequent Silurian and Devonian periods (438-360 million years ago), and many of them were heavily armored. These archaic armored agnathans, and early jawed fish known as placoderms, dominated the waters at first. Soon they were joined by apparently more modern-looking chondrichthyans (cartilaginous fishes), ancestors of modern sharks and rays; osteichthyans (bony fishes) appeared later, in Middle and Late Devonian times.

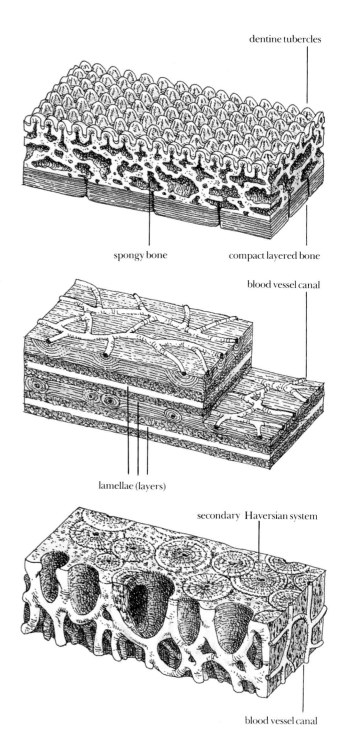

Block diagrams of three major types of bone. Aspidin (top) is typical of the bony armor of the early jawless fishes. Laminar bone (middle) is typical of many cold-blooded and smaller vertebrates. Haversian bone (bottom) is seen in the warm-blooded mammals and birds, and larger living reptiles, as well as in dinosaurs and other large extinct reptiles

The fishes closest to being amphibians? Two impressions of osteolepids from the Devonian of Scotland and Canada. The fossil skeleton of Osteolepis macrolepidotus *(below left) shows the bony scales and lobed lower fins. The model is of a relative,* Eusthenopteron *(below right). It is believed that the osteolepids could use their lobed fins for locomotion on land, as they dragged themselves from pool to pool.*

FISHES OF THE OLD RED SANDSTONE

The Old Red Sandstone of the Devonian period, from the north of Scotland, provides a magnificent "window" on these early fishes. The spectacular fossil specimens from Cromarty, Caithness, Morayshire, and Orkney attracted attention as early as 1825. Many leading geologists became deeply interested in the strange fish specimens that were collected there, partly because of their novelty, and partly because of their great age.

One of the most remarkable names associated with the Old Red fish is that of Hugh Miller (1802-56), the self-educated "stonemason of Cromarty." He worked as a mason, but also studied local natural history and geology in his spare time - such as it was. He collected specimens of the armored agnathans and placoderms, including forms such as *Pterichthyodes* and *Coccosteus*. By 1840, Miller had moved to Edinburgh, where he wrote *The Old Red Sandstone* (1841), which introduced the Old Red fish to an enthralled general public in a robust and lyrical style:

"The figure of the *Coccosteus* I would compare to a boy's kite ... There is a rounded head, a triangular body, a long tail attached to the apex of the triangle, and arms thin and rounded where they attach to the body, and spreading out towards their termination, like the ancient one-sided shovel which we see sculptured on old tombstones, or the rudder of an ancient galley. The manner in which the plates are arranged on the head is peculiarly beautiful; but I am afraid I cannot adequately describe them. A ring of plates, like the ring-stones of an arch, runs along what may be called the hoop of the kite ..."

Since 1840, many thousands of specimens of these fishes have come to light, and they indicate a diverse array of creatures preserved in the mudstones and siltstones of an ancient giant lake. Various small fishes fed on floating plants near the surface, and they were preyed on by carnivorous forms such as the placoderm *Coccosteus* and the bony fish *Cheirolepis*. The heavier placoderms such as *Pterichthyodes* scavenged for organic matter - decaying plant and animal remains - over the shallower parts of the lake bed.

Some of the most important Old Red fishes were the lobefins, a group that still survives today, but in much reduced numbers. Lobefinned fish such as *Dipterus* and *Osteolepis* fed on lakeside plants of the time such as mosses, horsetails, and scale trees, as well as the floating phytoplankton (plant plankton). The larger lobefin *Glyptolepis*, which reached lengths of over three feet (one metre), may have been a lurking predator like a modern pike, hiding among water plants and launching itself rapidly at passing prey. The lobefins, also known as sarcopterygians, are a group of bony fishes which have fleshy, muscular fins instead of the more usual "ray fins" of the actinopterygians, the familiar bony fishes such as herring, cod, tuna, carp, and salmon. Lobefins still surviving today include the lungfishes and the so-called living fossil *Latimeria*, the coelacanth. But they were much more significant in Devonian times, and they form a crucial link in the story of the evolution of vertebrates. They were the fishy ancestors of the first land vertebrates: the tetrapods.

EUSTHENOPTERON, THE ANCESTOR OF TETRAPODS?

Lobefins like Osteolepis, and its close relative *Eusthenopteron*, are generally reckoned to be similar to the hypothetical ancestor of the amphibians, the first tetrapods (four-limbed land animals). Eusthenopteron was a long, slender fish with a broad, three-pronged tail. The key areas of interest in studying such evolutionary connections are the skull and the paired fins underneath the body.

The skull is made up from numerous thin plates of bone that fit together in a regular pattern. The skull was flexible to some extent, as in most fishes, with hinge lines between the bones covering the top and the cheeks, and between the bones around the jaws and the rest of the skull. The key feature of the arrangement of Eusthenopteron's skull bones, which struck palaeontologists some time ago, was that it is virtually indistinguishable in many details from the arrangement seen in the first amphibians.

The pectoral fin (the fin beneath the "shoulder" region) of *Eusthenopteron* contains all the major bones seen in the front limb of a tetrapod: humerus (upper arm bone), radius, and ulna (forearm bones), wrist bones, and traces of a few finger structures. The correspondence is not exact, but many paleontologists believe that there is some measure of equivalence between the fish fin of Eusthenopteron and the land limb of an early amphibian. Yet if there was an evolutionary link between the two, how could the enormous leap be made between swimming and walking? This involved only one of a tremendous series of changes for life out of water.

PROBLEMS OF LIFE ON LAND

Many anatomical and physiological changes were needed in the fishy ancestors of the tetrapods, in order to guarantee success on the land. Not least was the ability to breathe in air. Also important were the changes in the skeleton and muscles. A body weighs much more in air than in water. Hence, the first amphibians needed a much stronger backbone, ribs, and other supporting bones than in any fish, simply to prevent the body from collapsing.

Moving also involved many alterations. Fish swim by smooth gliding motions produced by side-to-side undulations of the body and positional changes of the fins, whereas tetrapods move by separate footsteps which propel the body forward in a jerky fashion. It is possible that *Eusthenopteron*, like some modern lobefins, was able to use its muscular, paired, lobed fins to "walk," or at least pull itself, along the bottom of lakes. But it could not have walked on land. Detailed biomechanical studies of the well-preserved bones of

EUSTHENOPTERON

This osteolepid fish, up to three feet (one metre) long, is known from Late Devonian fresh-water deposits in Scotland and Canada. It was a powerful swimmer, evidenced by the deep three-part tail fin and the long narrow body. But it was probably also able to move about on land by a kind of "walking," in which it dragged its body along in the mud using its paired pectoral and pelvic fins.

THE EVOLUTION OF THE REPTILE LIMB

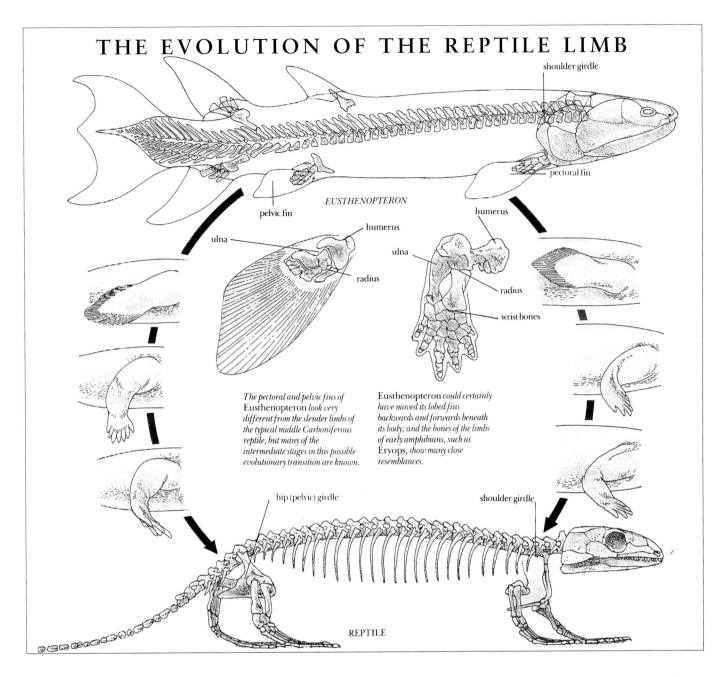

EUSTHENOPTERON

shoulder girdle

pectoral fin

pelvic fin

humerus

ulna

radius

humerus

ulna

radius

wrist bones

The pectoral and pelvic fins of Eusthenopteron *look very different from the slender limbs of the typical middle Carboniferous reptile, but many of the intermediate stages in this possible evolutionary transition are known.*

Eusthenopteron *could certainly have moved its lobed fins backwards and forwards beneath its body; and the bones of the limbs of early amphibians, such as* Eryops, *show many close resemblances.*

hip (pelvic) girdle

shoulder girdle

REPTILE

Eusthenopteron's shoulder and forelimb show that the fin pointed mainly backwards, and only a little sideways. The fin could have swung back and forth through only 20-25⁻ - not enough for true walking. The main motion was at the shoulder joint, with a very slight elbow bend.

As the amphibian limb evolved, the shoulder girdle had to be strengthened and separated from the back of the skull. Fishes have no neck, since their shoulder girdle bones are attached directly to the back of the skull. The arm bones had to lengthen, and the wrist and hand develop. In addition, the various joints along the arm

needed to become more flexible and stronger, along with the associated muscles needed for moving on land. In walking, the upper part of the amphibian limb moves back and forth in a roughly horizontal plane, while the lower portion of the arm swings from nearly horizontal to vertical, and then back to horizontal again, during the course of a stride. And, of course, all these changes were needed in the rear limbs, too.

Other problems of life on land are manifold, and they all had to be overcome: modifications to the mouth and digestion for new types of food; breathing air using lungs instead of gills; prevention of water loss through

FISHES FROM THE OLD RED SANDSTONE

Five fishes from the Old Red Sandstone of Scotland. The heavily armored placoderms Pterichthyodes (1) and Coccosteus (2), the former a mud-scavenger and the latter a carnivore, belong to an entirely extinct group. The other three are bony fishes, Cheirolepis (3) being not unlike some modern forms. Osteolepis (4) and Dipterus (5) belong to the lobe-finned group, close to the origin of the amphibians.

the skin, and when breathing; new sense organs that could work in air; and changes in the means of reproduction. In the face of all of these challenges, it may seem hard to understand why the lobefins ever bothered to venture onto land.

THE FIRST AMPHIBIANS

The oldest known amphibians are *Ichthyostega* and *Acanthostega*, from fossils in rocks of the Late Devonian (370 million years ago) in Greenland. Skeletons were first collected in the 1930s, and major new discoveries have been made recently. These are clearly land animals because of their well-developed limbs, reinforced backbone and ribs, and separation of the skull and shoulder girdle. However, the body outline is still streamlined as

in a fish, and there is a fish-like tail fin. No doubt *Ichthyostega* still spent a great deal of time in water, swimming by powerful sweeps of its tail, but it could waddle about on land. The weight of its large skull and massive rib cage probably meant that it would have had to rest its head and belly on the ground from time to time. However, fleetness of foot was probably not a priority at the time, since there were no large land predators. *Ichthyostega* fed on fish and probably also on the odd worm or millepede that it managed to overtake away from water.

But why move onto land in the first place? The "classical" theory, put forward by the American paleontologist Alfred Sherwood Romer, is that the lobefins took to the land in order to escape from the effects of drought and drying pools. Living lungfishes can survive for long

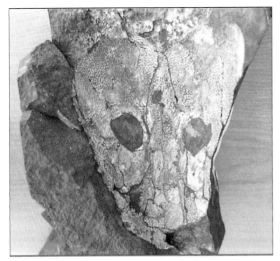

Spectacular new photographs of the oldest known land vertebrates, Ichthyostega (above left) and Acanthostega (above right and left), both from the Late Devonian of East Greenland. These photographs of the roofs of the skulls show that the pattern of bones is almost identical to that of their closest fishy relatives, the osteolepids. The shape and orientation of each skull can be made out by the position of the eye sockets, the large round openings in each specimen. The Ichthyostega skull is nearly complete, while those of Acanthostega are broken along the midline.

periods out of the water, and can even protect themselves buried in a "cocoon" during the dry period, until the next rainy season replenishes their ponds. The Devonian period also seems to have been arid at times, and fresh-water and shallow-water marine fishes might have been wiped out in mass killings when their ponds dried up. The lobefins had a slight edge in being able to breathe air and crawl short distances to other ponds. In other words, according to this theory, terrestrial locomotion evolved as a means of remaining in the water! However, a more recent view is that there is little evidence for this paradoxical idea.

The simplest hypothesis is that vertebrates moved to the land because there was a rich and as yet untapped source of food there. Plants, insects, spiders, and millepedes had conquered dry land much earlier, probably during the Silurian period (438-408 million years ago), and they were tolerably diverse by Late Devonian times. Sooner or later, it was inevitable that fish would start to exploit this new source of food, and they did so with increasing success as they evolved into amphibians, and then reptiles.

THE CARBONIFEROUS, THE AGE OF AMPHIBIANS

During the Carboniferous period (360-286 million years ago), the amphibians evolved rapidly and diversified into some 20 distinctive families. The Carboniferous is the famous age of great "coal forests," when a variety of giant clubmosses, 130-feet (40-metre) tall lycopod ferns, 50-feet (15-metre) horsetails, and ferns of other kinds formed great humid, tropical jungles over much of Europe and North America. These forests were inhabited by insects large and small, including dragonflies with the wingspan of a pigeon, as well as millepedes six feet (two metre) long, and also spiders, worms, and snails in the undergrowth. These rich habitats formed a diverse back-drop to the rise of the amphibians, and of course they provided the massive deposits of coal that still provide fuel in much of the northern hemisphere.

Most of the interesting Early Carboniferous amphibians have been found recently in several localities in Scotland by a professional fossil collector, Stan Wood. He explored old coal-bearing formations, abandoned mine heaps, and quarries, and came upon some amaz-

continued on page 30

CONTINENTAL DRIFT

The continents and oceans are not static. A growing body of evidence has shown that the Earth's crust is divided into a number of large plates that are in motion relative to each other, and have been throughout geological time.

The evidence for continental drift began to accumulate in the Middle Ages when Francis Bacon, the eminent philosopher and scientist, observed the apparent match between the coasts of Africa and South America, on either side of the South Atlantic Ocean.

In the early twentieth century, Alfred Wegener added further geological and paleoclimatological data. He noted that if the southern continents were pushed together, closing the Atlantic, Indian, and Antarctic Oceans, many geological formations from the Carboniferous and Permian periods matched closely across the modern continental margins. He also saw that the distribution of evidence for ancient climates, and the position of the ancient equator, only made sense if the continents had been arranged differently in the past.

Wegener was widely ridiculed at the time. However, observations on the floor of the Atlantic Ocean in the 1950s and 1960s showed how a new ocean crust was being formed along the Mid-Atlantic Ridge, hence pushing Europe and Africa away from the Americas. Continental drift was vindicated, and the processes of plate tectonics explained how it happened.

During the Carboniferous, the continents were moving together. During Permian and Triassic times, they amalgamated to form the supercontinent of Pangaea. Since then, the Atlantic Ocean has opened up, Australia and India have moved north, and Antarctica has moved to the South Pole.

CARBONIFEROUS

P[

TRIASSIC

J[

CRETACEOUS

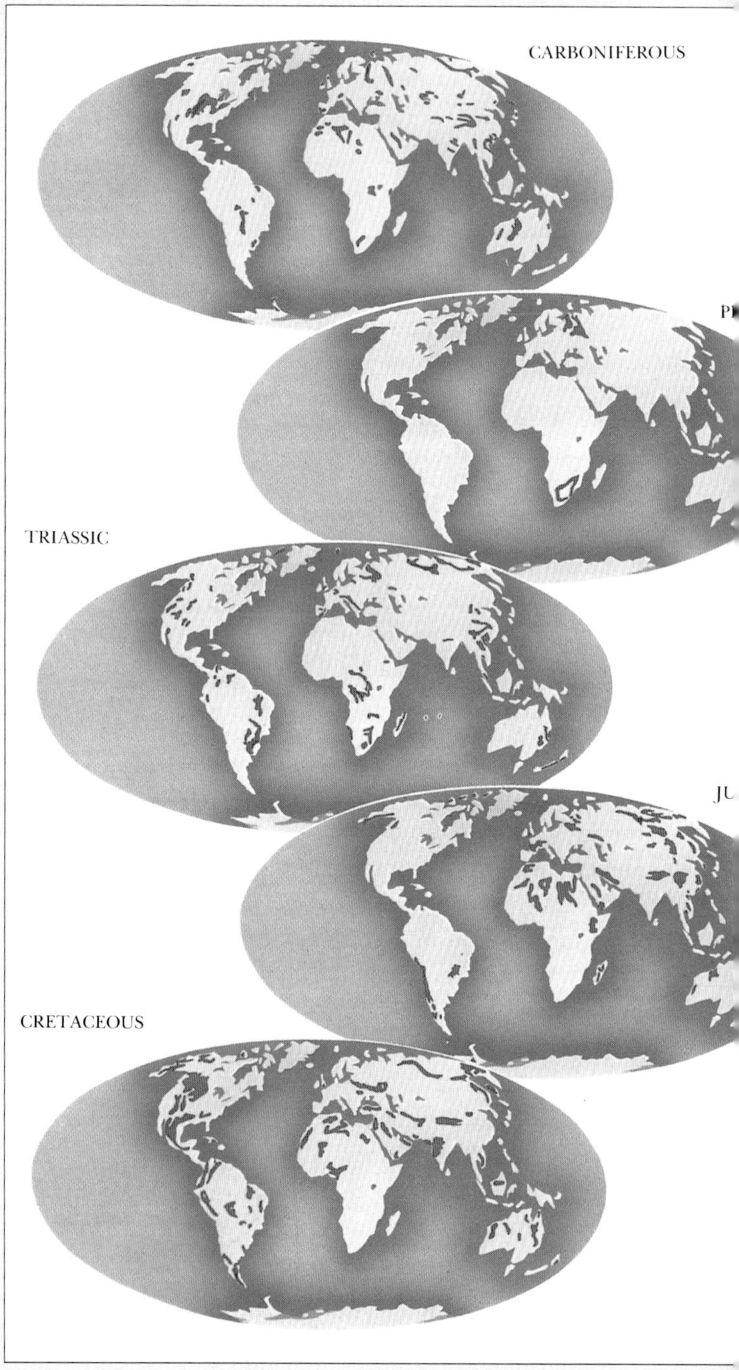

Far right: The continents as they appear in the relevant periods represented in this book. During the Carboniferous, the continents were moving together. During Permian and Triassic times, they amalgamated. Since then, the Atlantic Ocean has opened up, Australia and India have moved north, and Antarctica has moved to the South Pole.
Right: Where the various rock formations can be found today.

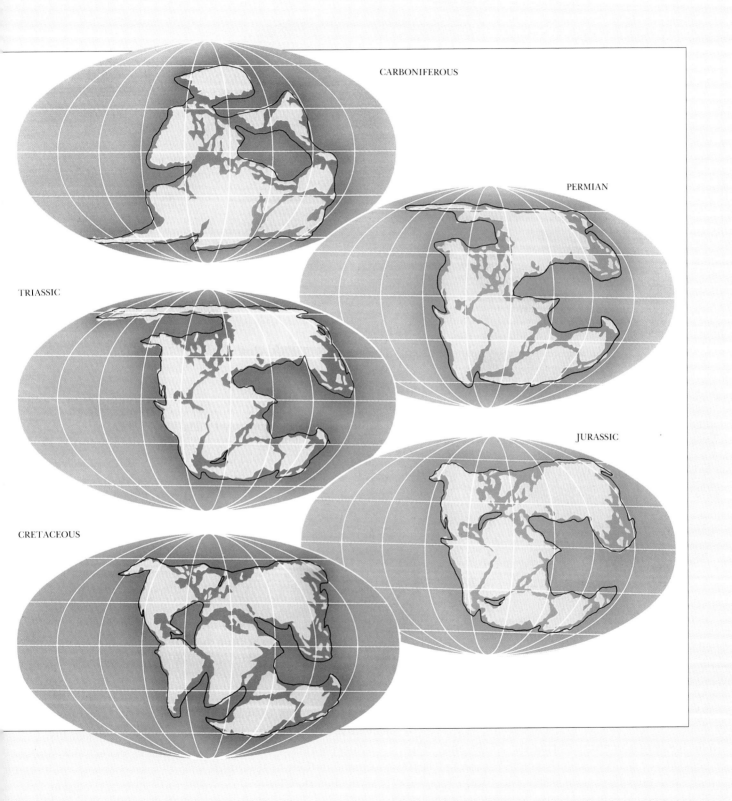

CARBONIFEROUS

PERMIAN

TRIASSIC

JURASSIC

CRETACEOUS

EOGYRINUS

Eogyrinus is a secondarily aquatic amphibian, known from the mid Carboniferous of England. It has an elongated, almost eel-like body, short limbs, and a long tail with a substantial tail fin. The limbs are too short, and too far apart, to support the body efficiently on land. Swimming was fish-like, by lateral undulations of the body and tail, and the limbs were used for steering.

The temnospondyl amphibian Eryops *(left) from the Early Permian of Texas. This fully terrestrial animal has a relatively short body and heavy limbs, although the latter would have permitted only short bursts of a rather lumbering gait. The head, remarkably, is as much as one-quarter of the body length, and the broad curving jaws are lined with dozens of small, sharp teeth. The skull is low, and there is every indication that* Eryops *was not over-endowed with brains!*

ingly fossil-rich deposits during the 1970s and 1980s. *Crassigyrinus* is a typical early amphibian, with a heavy skull, large jaws lined with sharp fangs, and a long narrow body but tiny limbs. This largely aquatic animal lived in large lakes and probably lurked among the tangles of vegetation and fallen trees on the bottom, where it sought fishes and possibly large invertebrates.

Another Early Carboniferous amphibian, *Proterogyrinus*, has been found in both North American and Scotland. Like many other such finds, it provides strong evidence that the Atlantic Ocean did not exist at that time. Carboniferous amphibians could wander freely across Europe and North America, since both continents were fused together as a single land mass, which broke up only later, during the Mesozoic – the age of dinosaurs. This is part of the well-known theory of continental drift, the strongly supported idea that the continents are all in (very slow) motion and that their distribution has never been static. *Proterogyrinus* seems to have been better adapted for life on the land than was *Crassigyrinus*, and it may have been able to walk fairly fast. However, its skull and teeth still indicate a mixed carnivorous diet of fish and land invertebrates. Other relatives of *Proterogyrinus*, known collectively as the anthracosaurs and including *Eogyrinus*, remained aquatic in their adaptations.

During the Late Carboniferous and subsequent

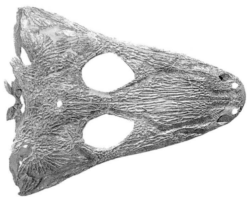

The temnospondyl amphibians survived through the Triassic period, but most disappeared before the dinosaurs began their main evolution. Typical Triassic forms include Plagiosuchus (above) and Capitosaurus (right), from Germany. Both were aquatic, as revealed by the well-marked channels on the skull bones, showing the location of the sensory lateral line canals.

Permian periods, the amphibians diverged into several distinctive groups. Some rather small types came on the scene, such as the nectrideans. A particularly unusual nectridean was Diplocaulus from the Early Permian of Oklahoma and Texas, which had a remarkably expanded skull equipped with two "horns" at the back that gave the head a boomerang shape. The outgrowths were formed from the normal skull bones, and not as the result of some peculiar disease or malformation. Their function has inevitably provoked considerable discussion among palaeontologists.

Numerous suggestions have been made for the "horns" of Diplocaulus: they protected sets of external gills, they accommodated throat pouches, they were counterbalances for the heavy head, they helped in defense, they assisted movement, they were used in pre-mating fights, and so on. Recent biomechanical studies, in which models of Diplocaulus heads were tested in a wind tunnel, have shown that the head acted like the wing of an airplane in providing lift. Flowing water and flowing air act in essentially the same way. Thus, under the influence of flowing water, the head would automatically tilt upwards. It has been suggested that Diplocaulus lurked on the bottom of slow-moving streams and that it caught fish swimming above, by lunging upward. A slight flick of the tail, and the current would tilt the head up ready to seize the fish. Diplocaulus would then sink back to the bottom to enjoy its feast.

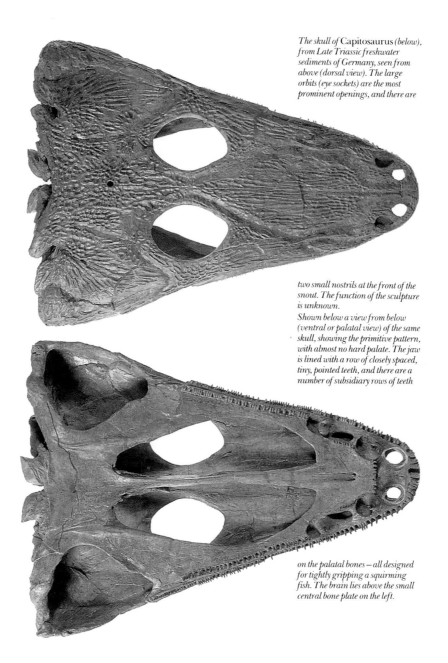

The skull of Capitosaurus *(below), from Late Triassic freshwater sediments of Germany, seen from above (dorsal view). The large orbits (eye sockets) are the most prominent openings, and there are*

two small nostrils at the front of the snout. The function of the sculpture is unknown.
Shown below a view from below (ventral or palatal view) of the same skull, showing the primitive pattern, with almost no hard palate. The jaw is lined with a row of closely spaced, tiny, pointed teeth, and there are a number of subsidiary rows of teeth

on the palatal bones — all designed for tightly gripping a squirming fish. The brain lies above the small central bone plate on the left.

The fossil record shows that some amphibian groups became rather more terrestrial in adaptations during the Late Carboniferous and Permian. Indeed some, such as the microsaurs, probably looked rather like the small lizards of today. The increasing terrestrialisation happened independently in three or four groups of amphibians, probably because the lush, humid coal forests were receding as arid conditions spread. Anatomical, physiological, and behavioral means were found by evolution to limit water loss from the body, to survive in drier conditions, and to move more rapidly in more open habitats, in order to escape from predators or catch prey. One amphibian group in particular is of interest here, since it gave rise to the first fully terrestrial vertebrates -the reptiles - during the Carboniferous period.

THE FIRST REPTILES

The oldest known reptile, until recently, was *Hylonomus* from the Mid Carboniferous rocks of Nova Scotia, Canada. This small animal, eight inches (20 centimeters) long, probably looked superficially like a lizard. It had a small, solid skull, a relatively long neck, long slender hands and feet, and a long thin tail. The

FISH AND AMPHIBIANS

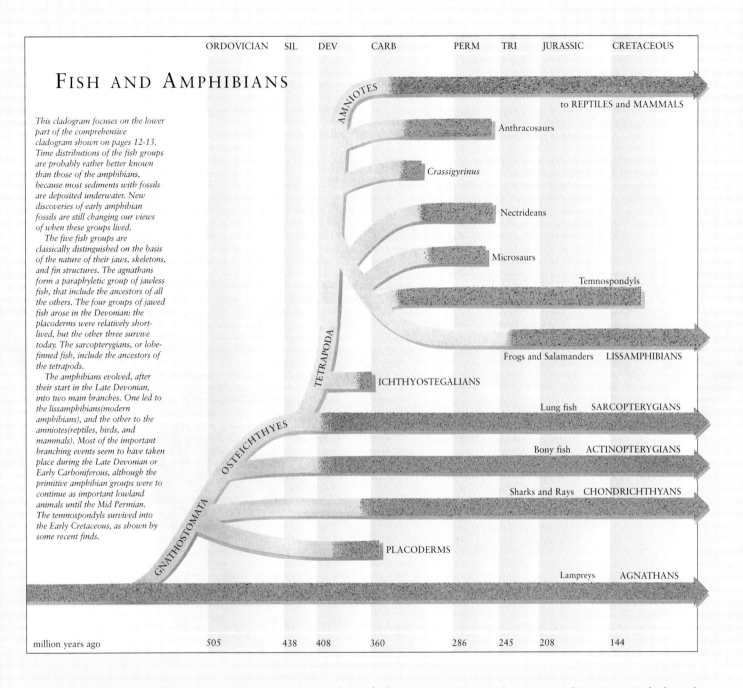

This cladogram focuses on the lower part of the comprehensive cladogram shown on pages 12-13. Time distributions of the fish groups are probably rather better known than those of the amphibians, because most sediments with fossils are deposited underwater. New discoveries of early amphibian fossils are still changing our views of when these groups lived.

The five fish groups are classically distinguished on the basis of the nature of their jaws, skeletons, and fin structures. The agnathans form a paraphyletic group of jawless fish, that include the ancestors of all the others. The four groups of jawed fish arose in the Devonian: the placoderms were relatively short-lived, but the other three survive today. The sarcopterygians, or lobe-finned fish, include the ancestors of the tetrapods.

The amphibians evolved, after their start in the Late Devonian, into two main branches. One led to the lissamphibians(modern amphibians), and the other to the amniotes(reptiles, birds, and mammals). Most of the important branching events seem to have taken place during the Late Devonian or Early Carboniferous, although the primitive amphibian groups were to continue as important lowland animals until the Mid Permian. The temnospondyls survived into the Early Cretaceous, as shown by some recent finds.

ORDOVICIAN SIL DEV CARB PERM TRI JURASSIC CRETACEOUS

AMNIOTES

to REPTILES and MAMMALS

Anthracosaurs

Crassigyrinus

Nectrideans

Microsaurs

Temnospondyls

Frogs and Salamanders LISSAMPHIBIANS

TETRAPODA

ICHTHYOSTEGALIANS

Lung fish SARCOPTERYGIANS

OSTEICHTHYES

Bony fish ACTINOPTERYGIANS

Sharks and Rays CHONDRICHTHYANS

GNATHOSTOMATA

PLACODERMS

Lampreys AGNATHANS

million years ago 505 438 408 360 286 245 208 144

bones of the skull, and the general proportions of the body, show that *Hylonomus* was an active land animal - a member of a new group that had progressed beyond the terrestrial amphibians in its adaptations.

The skull of *Hylonomus* is especially informative. In particular, the jaws are much stronger than those of a typical amphibian, both for biting and for retaining prey. Detailed biomechanical modelling has shown that *Hylonomus*, like other reptiles, could bite more firmly than an amphibian through the tough skin of an insect or millipede. In addition, having caught its prey, *Hylonomus* could have held it better and prevented it

from struggling and escaping: bear in mind that this lizard-sized reptile was feeding on cockroaches and similar insects as large as a child's hand!

Hylonomus fossils were found in mudstones, sandstones, and coal deposited in shallow fresh-water lakes and rivers. The skeletons are often in excellent condition because of a unique mode of preservation in fossilized tree stumps. The first such tree stumps were found in 1852 by the eminent Canadian palaeontologist William Dawson, and over 30 have been discovered since then. It seems that the Carboniferous scene in Nova Scotia was dominated by lush forests of the lycopod tree

One of the oldest reptiles, Paleothyris acadiana from the mid Carboniferous of Nova Scotia. The lower jaw lies on the right, the backbone curves up and down, and the back limbs stick out sideways on the left.

Sigillaria. Occasionally, the lakes flooded and inundated the forests. The trees were felled and the trunks washed away, leaving only the stumps rooted in the ground. Mud and sand built up around the stumps, and the internal woody tissue rotted away to leave a hollow cavern which acted as a kind of natural and very effective animal trap. Non-flying insects and other arthropods fell in, and so did a variety of small reptiles and amphibians. It seems that some *Hylonomus* specimens may have lived in the stumps, feeding on the millipedes, snails, and insects that were trapped there. However, eventually, the whole little community was entombed by the deposition of fresh sediment from above.

An important discovery made by the Scottish fossil collector Stan Wood in 1989 has now changed our perception of the origin of the reptiles. *Hylonomus* dates from about 310 million years ago, the beginning of the Late Carboniferous (Pennsylvanian) period. Wood uncovered a small reptile skeleton in one of his Scottish Early Carboniferous (Mississippian) localities dated at about 350 million years old. This discovery has pushed back the date of the origin of the reptiles, closer to the origin of the amphibians (370 million years ago?) than anyone had imagined possible. The significance of this new find awaits evaluation, since the specimen has not yet been studied in full. The affinities of the new Scottish reptile are not certain as yet. But *Hylonomus*, and other early reptiles, appear to be most closely related to the anthracosaur amphibians like *Proterogyrinus* and *Eogyrinus*, and possibly also *Crassigyrinus*.

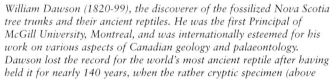

William Dawson (1820-99), the discoverer of the fossilized Nova Scotia tree trunks and their ancient reptiles. He was the first Principal of McGill University, Montreal, and was internationally esteemed for his work on various aspects of Canadian geology and palaeontology. Dawson lost the record for the world's most ancient reptile after having held it for nearly 140 years, when the rather cryptic specimen (above

right) was extracted from the Early Carboniferous of Scotland in 1989. It was found by Stan Wood, a renowned professional collector. The skull lies at the top right, and the backbone curves left and then down. A bent back limb is seen near the bottom left, and the tail runs down to the right.

Shortly after the origin of the amphibians, the tetrapod group split into two major branches. One led through the anthracosaurs to the reptiles, and eventually to birds and mammals. The other can be traced through various early amphibian groups, including the nectrideans and microsaurs, to the living amphibians –frogs, salamanders, and newts. These two branches of tetrapod evolution must have seemed equally significant during Early Carboniferous times, but the amphibians declined thereafter, while the reptiles burgeoned.

REPTILES AND AMPHIBIANS OF THE MID CARBONIFEROUS

A scene in the dank, humid coal forests of 320 million years ago, in Nova Scotia, Canada. A large aquatic amphibian, *Dendrerpeton*, swims in the lake. A giant dragonfly, more the size of a bird than an insect, flies across. Behind it, a giant eurypterid, 10 feet (three metres) long, hunts for prey.

In the foreground are some animals that give a fore-taste of things to come. They include three terrestrial microsaurs, an advanced group of amphibians; two are at bottom left, and one (at the bottom right) is about to fall into a tree-trunk hole, where it will be perfectly preserved. On the tree in front is *Hylonomus*, until recent ly one of the oldest known reptiles.

How the world looked in this period

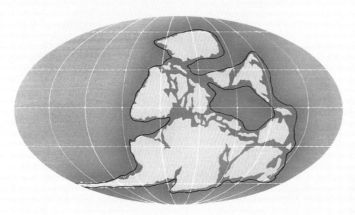

Dendrerpeton *(1), a bulky aquatic amphibian, was typical of many Carboniferous forms. One highly terrestrial group of amphibians were the microsaurs (2, 3, 4), which were rather smaller. The earliest reptiles, such as* Hylonomus *(5), looked superficially similar, but they arose from different amphibian ancestors.*

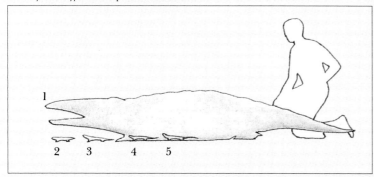

CHAPTER

THE REPTILES
TAKE OVER

After a modest beginning, the reptiles came to dominate the Permian scene. In particular, the mammal-like reptiles were the first major group to exploit the possibilities of a fully terrestrial existence. They included the famous sail-backed reptiles of the Early Permian, and the diverse and successful carnivorous and herbivorous forms of the Late Permian. Some of these were the first animals to achieve large size. Other innovations include the conquest of the sea by the mesosaurs, and the first flying vertebrates, the weigeltisaurs.

THE AMNIOTIC EGG, A "PRIVATE POND"

All the major reptilian lineages came on the scene during Late Carboniferous times, even though the amphibians still seemed to be the dominant animals in most parts of the world.

Reptiles owe their success to a variety of modifications to their anatomy, physiology, and behaviour, that set them apart from amphibians. Even the most terrestrial of amphibians must lay its eggs in water and cope with problems of water loss through the skin. The reptiles solved these problems most successfully.

The key feature of reptiles, and of their descendants the birds and mammals, is the amniotic or cleidoic ("closed") egg. Indeed, the amniotic egg defines the major evolutionary group known as the Amniota [Reptilia, Aves (Birds) and Mammalia], even though most mammals have since lost the eggshell by retaining the developing young animal within the body. Creatures in the Amniota group are known as amniotes.

The amniotic egg has both a shell or other tough outer coating that prevents water loss, and a series of internal membranes that protect the developing embryo, aid in its life processes, and collect waste products. The embryo floats in a protein-rich liquid called albumen, or egg white, and the whole egg can be regarded as an enclosed "private pond." It does not have to be laid in water since it encloses all the nutrients (in the yolk sac) and water that the developing animal needs. Amphibian eggs, such as frog spawn, are small and jelly-like, and they lack an outer covering. In air, they would dry out and die in a few minutes. Therefore, the amniotes finally broke the reproductive link with the fishy ancestry of the tetrapods some time during the Carboniferous period.

Amniotic eggs are larger than those of amphibians, and the parent generally lays far fewer than do amphibians or fish. The amniote strategy is to invest more reproductive energy and materials in each egg, and to protect the young from predation until a much later stage in their development. Amniotes have eliminated the larval, or tadpole, stage seen in the development of most fishes and amphibians.

Reproduction among amniotes takes place on dry

Supposedly the oldest known reptile egg (left), from the Admiral Formation (Early Permian) in Rattlesnake Canyon, Anchor County, Texas. Although the oldest reptile bones are now known from the Early Carboniferous, fossilised eggs have not been found from that time. This Permian specimen may be an egg – or, some suggest, merely a stony concretion.

Cast of the skeleton of a tiny primitive reptile, the herbivorous procolophonid Leptopleuron *from the Late Triassic of Scotland (below). The original fossil has been removed from the rock while it was buried, leaving a perfect "hole" or mould.*

land, so that internal fertilisation is essential; male fishes and amphibians generally shed their sperm into the water in the general direction of freshly laid eggs. When mating takes place on land, the male must deliver the sperm directly into the body of the female.

Fossil eggs are rare, and the oldest ones yet found come from well after the Carboniferous. The oldest supposed fossil egg has been reported from the Early Permian of Texas, but it may just as well be a calcareous concretion of nodule that formed by geological processes in the soil Unequivocal eggs become common only with the advent of the dinosaurs in the Mesozoic era, about 200 million years ago, from which numerous examples are known. Hence palaeontologists are faced with the rather unsatisfactory situation of attempting to chart the early evolution of amniotes in the absence of their key characteristic, the amniotic egg. How can we be sure *Hylonomus*, and the new Scottish find mentioned previously, are really reptiles?

OTHER AMNIOTIC INDICATORS

Various adaptive features have been proposed to identify early amniotes. For example, *Hylonomus* and other early supposed reptiles show major changes from the amphibians, both in the characters of the skull bones and in their body size. However, the simplest and most convincing argument comes from a cladistic view of tetrapod evolution, which hinges on the ancestry of a specific feature. Modern and fossil amniotes belonging to several diverse lineages - mammal-like reptiles, mammals, turtles, lizards, crocodilians, dinosaurs, and birds - all possess an identical type of amniotic egg. The likelihood that this complex structure arose only once in the course of evolution is great, and the likelihood that almost identical amniotic eggs evolved several times in separate groups is very small. Hence the common ancestor of all the amniotes must have possessed it. That

common ancestor can be found by tracking back along the diverging lineages, as shown by the fossil record, until they meet at one point; on an evolutionary diagram, that point lies close to *Hylonomus*, and no doubt to the new Scottish "reptile", in the Carboniferous. Everything in these evolutionary lines after this point must have had an amniotic egg, even if the eggs themselves have not yet been found as fossils.

THE FIRST AMNIOTE RADIATION

Three major reptilian types existed in the Late Carboniferous. First, there are the protorothyridids such as *Hylonomus* and *Paleothyris*, from the Late Carboniferous and Early Permian of North America and central Europe. They were small, agile insectivores, and seem to have survived virtually unchanged for some 30 million years or more. Their skulls were relatively solid, with no major openings in the cheek region behind the eye.

The second reptilian type of the Late Carboniferous is represented by *Petrolacosaurus* from Kansas. It looks like a protorothyridid at first sight: slender and long-limbed, with similar adaptations to eating insects. However, it is the herald of a second major group of reptiles, quite distinct from the protorothyridids, and the evidence is contained in a few seemingly unimportant features of the skull. In the palate (the roof of the mouth and base of the braincase), there is an extra opening through the bones beneath the orbit (eye socket). And in the cheek region, there are two clear openings - temporal fenestrae - that protorothyridids did not have.

The third reptilian group is typified by *Ophiacodon* from the Late Carboniferous and Early Permian rocks of New Mexico. It was bigger than the two reptiles just described, reaching a total body length of up to 10 feet

Ophiacodon uniformis (below) from the Late Carboniferous and Early Permian rocks of New Mexico.

PRIMITIVE REPTILES

This phylogenetic diagram shows the possible evolutionary relationships of the major groups of Carboniferous and Permian reptiles, plotted against a time scale. The known duration of each group is shown, as well as postulated lines of common ancestry.

After the origin of the amniotes (reptiles, birds, mammals) in the Early Carboniferous, there was a major diversification in the Late Carboniferous, which marked the fundamental splitting of the group. The first synapsid, anapsid, and diapsid reptiles became differentiated.

The synapsids are the mammal-like reptiles and their descendants, the mammals. The anapsids include various primitive groups and the turtles. The diapsids led ultimately to the lizards, snakes and crocodilians.

This cladogram shows in detail parts of the overview phylogenetic diagram on pages 12-13. Later diapsid evolution is illustrated on page 111.

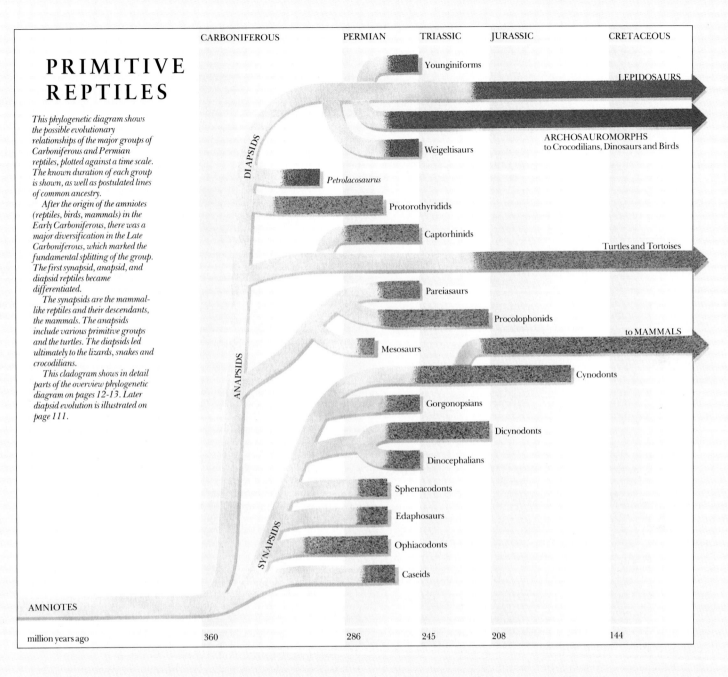

CARBONIFEROUS | PERMIAN | TRIASSIC | JURASSIC | CRETACEOUS

Younginiforms
LEPIDOSAURS
Weigeltisaurs
ARCHOSAUROMORPHS
to Crocodilians, Dinosaurs and Birds
DIAPSIDS
Petrolacosaurus
Protorothyridids
Captorhinids
Turtles and Tortoises
Pareiasaurs
Procolophonids
ANAPSIDS
Mesosaurs
to MAMMALS
Cynodonts
Gorgonopsians
Dicynodonts
Dinocephalians
Sphenacodonts
Edaphosaurs
SYNAPSIDS
Ophiacodonts
Caseids
AMNIOTES

million years ago | 360 | 286 | 245 | 208 | 144

(three metres). The skull is large compared to the body, and the remarkable high-sided snout makes up more than half of its length. *Ophiacodon* was clearly a carnivore, and it may have fed on fishes - and, indeed, other smaller tetrapods such as those described above. Again, the key to the evolutionary significance of *Ophiacodon* lies in the cheek region where there is a single temporal fenestra, possibly equivalent to the lower of the two seen in *Petrolacosaurus*.

These three reptiles indicate the three major lineages of amniote evolution that have dominated the Earth from 300 millions years ago to the present day. The key

to their identification lies in the skull "windows," the temporal fenestrae, which form a simple key to relationships, as follows.

The protorothyridids have no temporal fenestrae. This is the primitive anapsid ("no windows") condition seen in amphibians and reptiles. *Petrolacosaurus* is a diapsid ("two windows") reptile since it has two temporal fenestrae on each side of the skull. *Ophiacodon* is a synapsid ("joined-together windows") reptile. (A fourth type of skull, found in some diverse marine reptiles of the Mesozoic era, is the euryapsid ("wide window") form, but this does not seem to represent a single major amniote lineage.)

How can we resolve the relationships of the three major lineages from the Late Carboniferous? There are three possible evolutionary arrangements of the three groups: pair the diapsids and synapsids, the diapsids and anapsids or the anapsids and synapsids. The last possibility has not been considered seriously for other reasons, but the first two have their supporters. It might seem, with the abundance of evidence from fossils and living animals, that there should be no problem in resolving an evolutionary question as fundamental as this. And fundamental it is, since the skull fenestrae are vital clues in interpreting the relationships of the thousands of fossils. But it is not easy to decide whether the ultimate ancestors of modern lizards, crocodilians, and birds - all diapsids like Petrolacosaurus – are more closely related to the mammal's ultimate ancestors (synapsids like Ophiacodon), or to anapsids such as the protorothyridids. The evidence is not strong, but on balance it seems to support the later alternative. Hence we assume that the first split among the amniotes was between the synapsids on the one hand, and the anapsids and diapsids on the other.

THE PELYCOSAURS: SAIL-BACKED SYNAPSIDS

Toward the end of the Carboniferous period, and during the Early Permian, climates in the northern hemisphere, at least, became hot and arid in many parts. Extensive salt deposits formed in North America and across western and central Europe. The lush, damp, tropical Carboniferous coal swamps disappeared, and their dominant clubmoss and horsetail vegetation was replaced by seed-bearing plants of more modern types, such as conifers in the northern hemisphere. These new, drier landscapes came to be dominated by the synapsids, and in particular by a diverse group of synapsids called the pelycosaurs.

Pelycosaurs are best known from the extensive. Early Permian "red beds" of Texas and Oklahoma. Specimens have also been found in other parts of North America and in Europe. There were five families, of which two - caseids and edaphosaurs – were herbivorous.

One of the most remarkable caseids was *Cotylorhynchus*, the largest pelycosaur at a length of 10 feet (three metres), but equipped with a startlingly small head. Indeed, the skull is so small that it looks as if it belongs to an animal about one-quarter the size!

Cotylorhynchus has greatly enlarged nostrils, a pointed snout, and reduced teeth. It was clearly a herbivore, since the teeth are flattened and "spatulate" in shape rather than pointed, and they have crinkled edges which are adapted for cutting leaves, but which could not tear flesh. In addition, the jaw joint is placed below the level of the tooth rows, instead of being in line with them -an adaptation that gives greater strength to the jaw-closing muscles. Finally, *Cotylorhynchus* had a massive barrel-shaped rib cage that presumably contained the vast digestive system necessary for dealing with large quantities of tough plant food. (Meat is more digestible than vegetation, and carnivores have shorter intestines than herbivores.)

The second family of herbivorous pelycosaurs, the edaphosaurids, included *Edaphosaurus* from the Early Permian of New Mexico and Texas. Like *Cotylorhynchus*, its skull is relatively small in comparison to the body, the teeth are peg-like, and the lower jaw is deep. In addition, *Edaphosaurus* has an extensive "pavement" of teeth on the bones of the palate, which it presumably used, in conjunction with its scaly tongue, to grind up rough plant food.

However, the most striking feature of *Edaphosaurus* is the tall "sail" that runs down the middle of its back. This sail is composed of greatly elongated spines, each one the neural spine of one vertebra (backbone), which were doubtless covered with skin in life. The sail is seen in some other pelycosaurs as well.

SAILS AND TEMPERATURE CONTROL

Most pelycosaurs were carnivorous, and most did not have a sail. However, one member of the sphenacodontid family. *Dimetrodon* (from the Early Permian of Texas, New Mexico, and Oklahoma), is probably even better known than *Edaphosaurus* for this amazing dorsal structure.

Dimetrodon reached a total length of 10 feet (three metres) and had a relatively much larger skull than the herbivorous pelycosaurs. The massive fangs show that this animal was an effective top carnivore that probably fed on smaller pelycosaurs, and on amphibians and reptiles whose fossils have been found in the same rocks. The sail, like that of *Edaphosaurus*, was borne on long neural spines projecting from the top of the vertebrae. The length of the spines increased progressively from the neck to the middle of the reptile's back, and then

continued on page 46

The skeleton of Dimetrodon (from the Early Permian of Texas, New Mexico, and Oklahoma) shows off its amazing dorsal structure. There has been considerable debate about the function of this structure. Some scientists suggest it was used in mating displays, others suggest that it was coloured in irregular blotches for camouflage. However, the most likely suggestion is that the sail functioned in temperature control.

EARLY REPTILE DIVERSITY

The reptiles of the Carboniferous and Permian had already mapped out the major lines of evolution that were to be followed through the next 250 million years, to the present day. The captorhinomorphs, petrolacosaurs, and mammal-like reptiles are close to the ancestors of all later significant groups of reptiles, birds, and mammals.

The great diversification took place in the Mid to Late Carboniferous, probably soon after the origin of the reptiles. The key distinguishing features, which may be discerned from the start, are in the posterior part of the skull, when seen in side view.

The basic reptilian pattern, the anapsid condition, was to have no skull openings behind the eye socket. The other two major skull types, diapsid and synapsid, are characterised by two and one lower temporal "windows" (fenestrae) respectively. These are skull openings behind the eye socket that were associated with jaw muscle attachments. The fourth skull pattern, euryapsid, with a single upper temporal fenestra, is a later modification of the diapsid pattern found in several groups of marine reptiles.

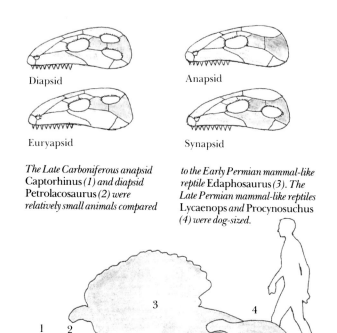

Diapsid

Anapsid

Euryapsid

Synapsid

The Late Carboniferous anapsid Captorhinus *(1) and diapsid* Petrolacosaurus *(2) were relatively small animals compared* *to the Early Permian mammal-like reptile* Edaphosaurus *(3). The Late Permian mammal-like reptiles* Lycaenops *and* Procynosuchus *(4) were dog-sized.*

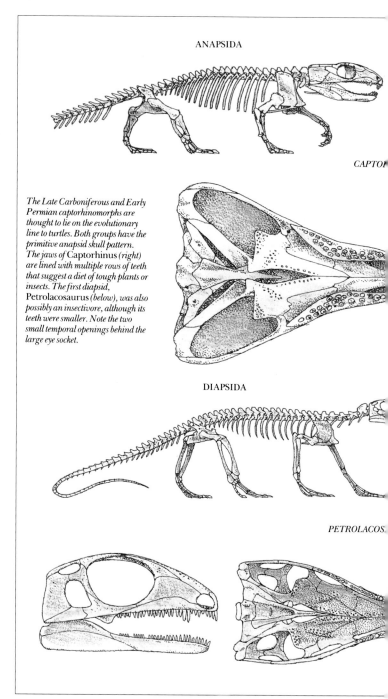

ANAPSIDA

CAPTOR

The Late Carboniferous and Early Permian captorhinomorphs are thought to lie on the evolutionary line to turtles. Both groups have the primitive anapsid skull pattern. The jaws of Captorhinus *(right) are lined with multiple rows of teeth that suggest a diet of tough plants or insects. The first diapsid,* Petrolacosaurus *(below), was also possibly an insectivore, although its teeth were smaller. Note the two small temporal openings behind the large eye socket.*

DIAPSIDA

PETROLACOS.

SYNAPSIDA

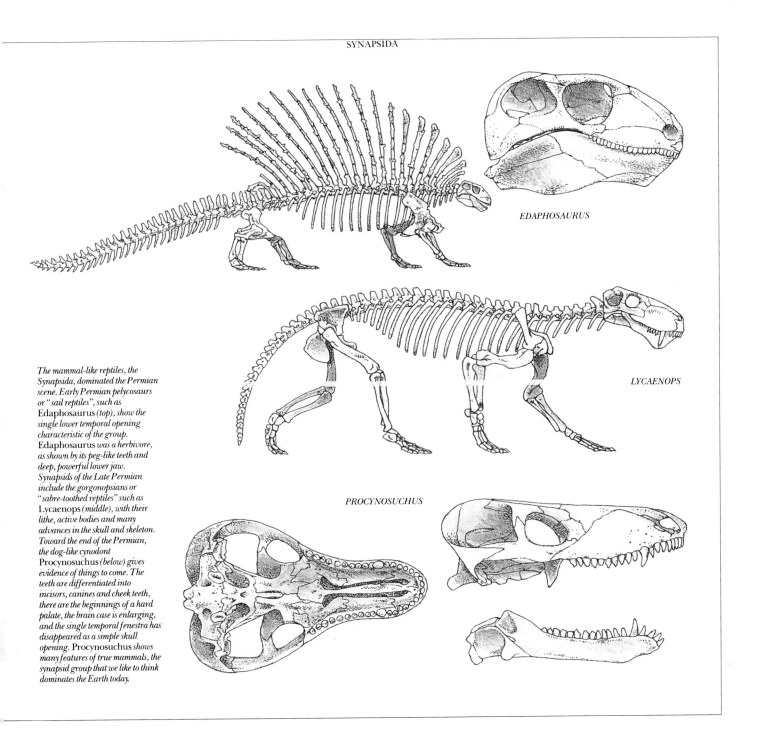

EDAPHOSAURUS

LYCAENOPS

PROCYNOSUCHUS

The mammal-like reptiles, the Synapsida, dominated the Permian scene. Early Permian pelycosaurs or "sail reptiles", such as Edaphosaurus (top), show the single lower temporal opening characteristic of the group. Edaphosaurus was a herbivore, as shown by its peg-like teeth and deep, powerful lower jaw. Synapsids of the Late Permian include the gorgonopsians or "sabre-toothed reptiles" such as Lycaenops (middle), with their lithe, active bodies and many advances in the skull and skeleton. Toward the end of the Permian, the dog-like cynodont Procynosuchus (below) gives evidence of things to come. The teeth are differentiated into incisors, canines and cheek teeth, there are the beginnings of a hard palate, the brain case is enlarging, and the single temporal fenestra has disappeared as a simple skull opening. Procynosuchus shows many features of true mammals, the synapsid group that we like to think dominates the Earth today.

mens of *Dimetrodon*, from juveniles to ..s the animal grew, the sail increased in size a faster rate than did the body length. This uggests the sail had some physiological function that may be explained by a basic biological principle: the relationship between body volume and surface area.

As animals become larger, their volume increases in relation to the cube (third power) of their body length. Their surface area increases as the square (second power). This, of course, reflects the fact at volume is a three-dimensional measure, ile area is two-dimensional and length has limension. Since the sail area is proportion-ody volume rather than to body area or

The skull (above) of Dimetrodon, with long teeth and deep jaws.

Edaphosaurus (below) was a herbivore unlike its meat-eating counterpart - Dimetrodon.

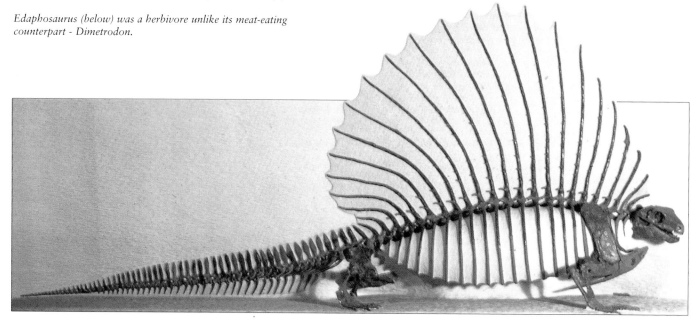

declined gradually toward the hip region. In side view, the sail had a smooth curved shape. But what was its function?

There has been a considerable amount of speculation about the possible functions of the pelycosaur sail. Some palaeobiologists suggest that it was used in pre-mating displays, or that it was coloured in irregular blotches for camouflage. However, the most popular suggestion is that the sail functioned in temperature control. Apparently, the size of the sail is related to the estimated body weight of the animal rather than to its body length. This has been established by looking at

length, then a strong connection is suggested with the physiology of temperature or water control. The former seems most likely, and a simple temperature regulation model has been developed to explain the function of the pelycosaur sail.

The pelycosaurs, like modern reptiles, were probably ectotherms. This means they did not generate much heat within their bodies, as endotherms like birds and mammals do. They had to rely on external means of controlling their internal temperatures. During the night, the body temperature of *Dimetrodon* fell to something approaching the cool air, much too low for rapid movement. As the sun rose in the morning, *Dimetrodon* probably crawled out onto an exposed area, in order to bask in the sun and raise its body temperature to a level suitable for activity. Without a sail, it has been calculated that it would take four times as long for *Dimetrodon* to raise its body temperature by 42°F (5°C). The sail was well supplied with blood vessels, shown by grooves on the surfaces of the supporting neural spines. It would have been an effective heat exchanger, picking up warmth from the sun and passing it, via the bloodstream, to the rest of the body. Thus *Dimetrodon* could have passed from nigh-time torpor to daytime activity more rapidly than if it lacked the sail, and this may have given it a significant advantage in capturing still-torpid prey that lacked sails. In the heat of the day, the sail may have been employed in reverse, as a rapid means of dissipating heat to prevent the animal from overheating.

The sail of the herbivore *Edaphosaurus* can then be seen as an adaptation to beat *Dimetrodon* at its own game. However, the story is not quite as simple as it seems. Most pelycosaurs and their contemporaries lacked sails, and yet they seemed to survive quite well enough!

THE RULE OF THE THERAPSIDS

The pelycosaurs disappeared soon after the end of the Early Permian. They seem to have been replaced worldwide by their descendants, a diverse synapsid group called the therapsids.

The function of the sail as a heat-exchanger in Edaphosaurus and Dimetrodon. The sail was covered in skin which contained many blood vessels. The theory is that the pelycosaur stood sideways to the sun in the morning, in order to speed its body warming after the cool night. It faced the sun in the heat of the day, with the sail end-on, in order to cool off.

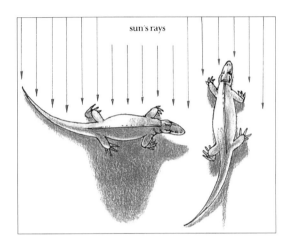

DIMETRODON

The most famous pelycosaur, Dimetrodon, *was a sphenacodont and the carnivorous counterpart of* Edaphosaurus. *It was also equipped with a very similar sail. However, there is no doubt that the sail in both animals evolved quite independently; the internal structure of the bony supports is entirely different. Since the sail occurred only in certain pelycosaurs and was found in both carnivores and herbivores, it must have bestowed some adaptive advantage on both.*

Therapsids differ from pelycosaurs in having a more advanced jaw apparatus and limbs. Late Permian therapsids are best known from the western U.S.S.R. and South Africa, where sequences of fossils have been excavated. For the first time, reptiles were the dominant animals - there were hardly any amphibians. Each of the faunas (assemblages of animals) contains 15-20 different species, ranging in size from a mouse to a hippo, and in habits from being semi-aquatic to terrestrial and even aerial. These are the first communities of amniotic animals that can be compared in any serious way to our modern communities.

The dinocephalians were a mixed group of carnivorous and herbivorous therapsids. *Titanosuchus* from South Africa, a typical carnivore, was dog-like in form, but had much shorter limbs and a heavier skull. The incisor teeth (those at the very front of the mouth) and the canines (fangs) were well developed, while the cheek teeth were sharply ridged, as in modern carnivorous mammals, for tearing flesh and shearing bones.

The skeletons of two dinocephalian mammal-like reptiles, the giant herbivore *Moschops* and the smaller carnivore *Titanosuchus*. Despite their great difference in size and appearance, both animals shared a similar skull and skeletal structure, and they dominated many Late Permian faunas.

The herbivorous dinocephalians were more unusual in appearance than their carnivorous cousins. Some,

such as *Moschops* (also from South Africa), were quite preposterous. This large reptile, 17 feet (five metres) long, had a massive rib cage and heavy limbs, but tiny hands and feet. The head was relatively small compared to the size of the body, as in the herbivorous pelycosaurs, and the neck was massively powerful. The skull had the unusual feature of a heavily built roof, up to four inches (10 centimetres) thick in some specimens. The only function that could be suggested for this enormously overgrown skull is that it was used in head-butting, in some way analogous to the way modern sheep and deer use their horns and antlers in pre-mating trials of strength between males. In *Moschops*, the main force of the butt hit the skull's thickened roof shield and was transmitted along thickened girders of bone to the neck, thus protecting the brain (such as it was); the shock then passed into the heavily muscled shoulders which provided much of the force for the initial charge.

THE DICYNODONT THERAPSIDS

The dominant herbivorous animals during the Late Permian, and indeed for much of the Triassic, were the dicynodonts. These therapsids are characterised by the loss of teeth: some forms have none at all, while others retain only two canines (dicynodont means "two-dog-toothed"). It may seem inexplicable that a group of toothless animals could be successful as herbivores.

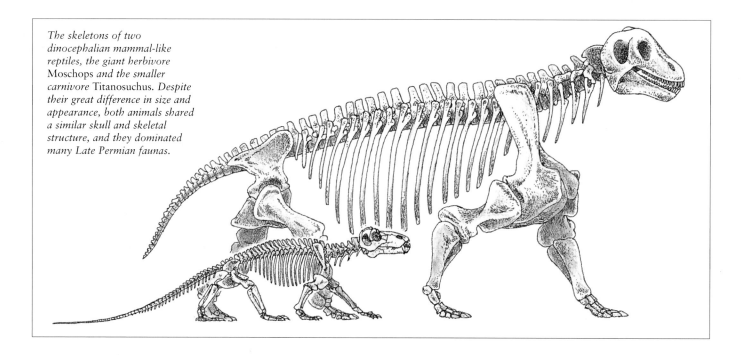

The skeletons of two dinocephalian mammal-like reptiles, the giant herbivore Moschops *and the smaller carnivore* Titanosuchus. *Despite their great difference in size and appearance, both animals shared a similar skull and skeletal structure, and they dominated many Late Permian faunas.*

The heavily built dinocephalian Tapinocephalus (above), showing the sprawling posture.

However, there is strong evidence that the fossilised jaws were covered in life by a scaly beak, just as in turtles and birds, which could be just as effective as a full set of teeth in cutting and crushing plant stems and leaves. *Endothiodon* was a moderately sized primitive dicynodont from South Africa, although its relatives ranged in size from an inch or so to about 10 feet (three meters).

Detailed studies of how the jaws worked show that *Endothiodon* and its relatives moved the lower jaw in a counterclockwise rotation, when viewed from the right side. When feeding, *Endothiodon* opened its jaws and pulled some leaves into the mouth, using its tongue and

The ecological importance of the major reptile groups (right) varied greatly through time.

palate. The lower jaw then slid forward, moved up to the closed position while grasping the plant material firmly in the beak, and then dragged the lower jaw back in contact with the upper jaw. This last movement firmly bit through even tough vegetable matter and cut it into pieces small enough for swallowing. Of course, Endothiodon, like all reptiles, could not chew its food in the way that mammals do. The food was swallowed in large chunks and broken down further within the stomach. A herd of feeding Endothiodon would no doubt have emitted an array of digestive noises!

THE FIRST "SABRE-TOOTHS"

Some of the dinocephalians were carnivorous, as noted above, but the dominant carnivores of the Late Permian were the gorgonopsians, such as *Lycaenops* from South Africa. This animal had a heavy skull and a prominent canine tooth in each side of the jaw. It could open its mouth by dropping the lower jaw to give an enormous gape of 90° or so, in order to clear the canines and make them ready for piercing the thick hide of its prey. In many ways, it seems that Lycaenops and its relatives were reptilian "sabre-toothed cats" of the Late Permian, anticipating the adaptations of those mammals by 250 million years. Large herbivores such as *Moschops* and certain dicynodonts no doubt had thick leathery skin, like modern rhinos and hippos, and sabre teeth were required to attack them effectively.

Lycaenops probably leapt at its prey animal, sank its

continued on page 52

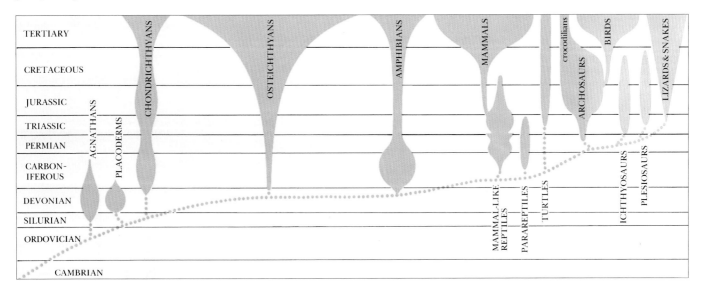

REPTILES OF THE LATE PERMIAN

This scene in southern Africa shows the diversity of typical Late Permian reptiles. In an arid landscape, the scene is dominated by small, medium, and large mammal-like reptiles. They include a trio of herbivorous dinocephalians, *Moschops*, on the right; the herbivorous dicynodont, *Dicynodon*, in front of them; and the carnivorous dinocephalian, *Titanosuchus* (middle), and gorgonopsians *Lycaenops* (left).

The other reptiles shown are diapsids - a superficially lizard-like *Youngina* (far right), climbing the trunk of a tree, and the gliding *Coelurosauravus* (top right and bottom left).

The world as it was then

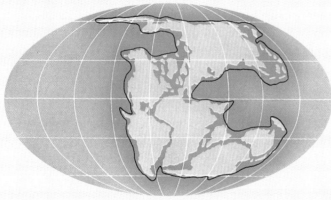

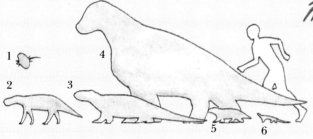

The Late Permian terrestrial reptiles show a broad range of sizes, from the tiny gliding Coelurosauravus (1), and the moderate-sized synapsids Titanosuchus (2) and Lycaenops (3), to the very large Moschops (4). Some of the most common herbivores were the medium-sized dicynodonts like Dicynodon (5), while many diapsids, like Youngina (6), were much smaller.

DICYNODONT FEEDING

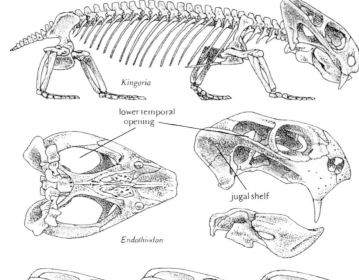

lower temporal opening

jugal shelf

Endothiodon

The Late Permian Kingoria has a skeleton (top) typical of most medium-sized dicynodonts. Its relative Endothiodon has a skull (left) that shows the large lower temporal opening and sweeping jugal shelf seen in all dicynodonts. Its biting and chewing cycle (below) has been worked out in some detail. It shows that the lower jaw moved in a broad circular movement, seizing a piece of plant food in the tip of the jaws, and tearing it backwards.

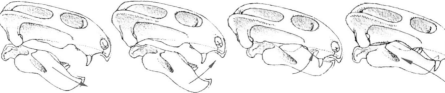

The skulls of two dicynodonts, showing their unusual shared characters of general toothlessness (barring the single canine on each side), the sharp beak, and the short, deep lower jaw. The skulls are of Diictodon sollasi (top) and Dicynodon feliceps (above), both from the Upper Cistecephalus Zone (Late Permian) of South Africa. The jaw joint is of crucial importance: it is set about half-way along the skull, under the eye, rather than right at the back. This provides a more powerful bite. The joint is roller-like, and the lower jaw can slip backwards and forwards, as well as hinge up and down.

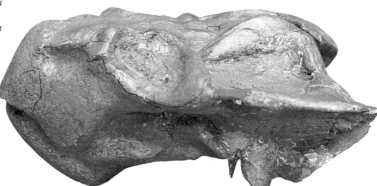

The skull of Oudenodon, a Late Permian dicynodont from South Africa (left). This specimen is shown roughly as it was picked up, eroded from the rock and lying exposed on the surface. The "beak" and lower jaw are clear, as are the circular eye socket and the larger temporal opening.

canines into the flanks or side of the neck, and clamped the jaws partly shut so that the points of the canines of the upper and lower jaws passed each other but did not touch. The incisors then interlocked, and Lycaenops tore off a chunk of flesh, thus disabling the victim, which may well have been appreciably larger than its predator.

Other therapsid groups were present in Late Permian times, mostly small to medium-sized carnivores. One such animal is *Procynosuchus*, also from South Africa, and a member of the cynodont reptiles. It is significant since it shows a number of rather mammalian charac-

ters when compared with its related contemporaries, such as clearly differentiated teeth (incisors, canines, cheek teeth), the beginnings of a secondary palate (that is, the true hard palate that we have in the roofs of our mouths, absent in most reptiles), and an advanced dog-like lower jaw.

THE KARROO BASIN AND ITS REPTILES

One of the most productive areas for therapsid reptile fossils has been the Karroo Basin of South Africa, an enormous complex of sandstones and mudstones laid down during the Late Permian, Triassic, and Early Jurassic - a total time span of 90 million years or more. The Karroo has yielded thousands of therapsid skulls from three major time periods, or horizons, covering much of the Late Permian. The first collections of Karroo reptiles were made in the 1840s by Andrew Geddes Bain (1797-1864), a Scottish engineer who worked building roads in Cape Colony. He went on fossil collecting trips and eventually found what he called a "charnel house," consisting of the bones of hundreds of reptiles.

Some of the most puzzling of Bain's discoveries were the dicynodont skulls. He thought at first that they must be the remains of tigers because of the pair of large fangs, but on closer inspection he could see that they bore no other similarities. The deeply religious local Boer farmers were interested in his discoveries and extremely puzzled about what they were. Once, Bain was excavating a large therapsid skeleton, about the size of a cow, and a young Boer asked him what he was doing:

"I said in reply to the Boer's query: "Don't you see that it is the petrified head of a wildebeest," pointing at the same time to the open mouth containing the teeth.

"Alamagtig," said he, his eyes glistening in astonishment, "how came the wildebeest in the stone?"

"Do you read your Bible?" said I.

"Oh yes."

'Well, did you never read that when Noah was in the ark (which contained a pair of all the different animals on the face of the earth) that one of the wildebeest jumped overboard, and before Noah could get out his life-buoy it was drowned?"

The poor Boer at first looked bewildered, but not wishing to be thought deficient in Bible lore, scratching his head and looking as sheepishly as possible, said: "Ja tog." (Yes, I remember.)

"Well, then," continued I, "you know of course that the waters covered the tops of the highest mountains, and that at that time Noah was floating above the lofty Winterberg, and the wildebeest, falling into the Fishback, became petrified there, where he has lain ever

The skull of the carnivorous gorgonopsian Lycaenops from South Africa. The gorgonopsians were the top carnivores of the Late Permian, feeding on the thick-skinned dicynodonts, dinocephalians, and pareiasaurs. They had a small number of long sharp teeth, including a pair of massive canines - real sabre teeth! The snout is narrow and deep.

The first of a key therapsid group, Procynosuchus, *from the latest Permian of South Africa. This is the skull of a carnivore, ancestor of the cynodonts and - ultimately - of the mammals.*
The teeth are differentiated into incisors (front), canines, and cheek teeth (molars).

since till I took him out the day before yesterday."

"Alamagtig," said the Boer again, "het is tog wonderlijk, (it is wonderful) and saddled up his horse and rode away."

Bain sent 40 or so skulls to the British Museum in London, where Sir Richard Owen (1804-92), at that time the leading British palaeontologist and anatomist, named them *Dicynodon*. However, he was in considerable confusion, as Bain had been, as to the true affinities of these remarkable fossils. In his description of 1845, Owen argued that the skulls were essentially lizard-like in appearance, but that the dentition was mammalian.

During the rest of the nineteenth century, more therapsid skulls were sent to London, where palaeontologists built up a fuller, but still patchy, understanding of their true diversity.

This changed when Robert Broom (1866-1951), another Scot, moved to South Africa and began a practice as a country doctor. He began collecting in the Karroo and amassed thousands of specimens which formed the nucleus of the major collections now held in several institutions in southern Africa. Broom built up a reputation as a fast worker with a wide scope of interests - he named hundreds of new species of therapsids during his career of over 50 years in southern Africa (although many have since turned out to be identical to other specimens already named!). Later, he turned his attention to collecting the remains of early humans. The image of Broom retained by many who collected with him in the field is of a Victorian who had survived

long into the twentieth century. His standard collecting outfit consisted of a top hat, tailcoat, and high starched collar.

Broom's legacy from his days in the Karroo Basin is a large collection of extremely important therapsid finds, and also the remains of a number of other non-therapsid reptiles which occurred with them.

THE NON-THERAPSIDS OF THE PERMIAN

Numerous anapsid groups came and went during the Permian, and it has so far proved difficult to establish their relationships, either to each other or to the more important lineages. The captorhinids, for example, were a diverse group that existed for most of the Permian, but whose origins are uncertain. They may be related to the turtles.

Captorhinus itself, from the Early Permian of Oklahoma, was a small animal with a relatively large skull. The key captorhinid features are seen in the dentition. The bone at the front of the skull, the premaxilla, bends down slightly and bears a few long teeth; the maxilla, the main toothbearing bone behind, is equipped with numerous smaller, peg-like teeth arranged in five or six multiple rows, that seem to slope diagonally across the width of the jaw. Some later captorhinids were much larger and had up to 12 separate rows of maxillary teeth.

It is not known whether the captorhinids used their striking dental equipment for crushing the hard cuticles of insects or tough plant materials.

Skull of the therocephalian
Zinnosaurus *(right), a*
moderate-sized carnivorous
therapsid. The snout is
long and high, as in the
gorgonopsians, and the eye
socket is set far back. The
long, narrow lower jaw is
adapted for shutting with
great speed, rather than
with particular strength.

The skull and partial skeleton of the small Late
Permian carnivore Ictidosuchops *(below. The*
bones behind the skull include vertebrae and
parts of the front limb and shoulder girdle.

Two skeletons of the small dicynodont Diictodon
entwined on a slab (above). These two may have
been buried while they slept, hence leaving the
bodies curled up and undisturbed.

Another unusual group of small anapsid reptiles are the procolophonids, which arose in the Late Permian. Procolophon, from the Early Triassic of South Africa and Antarctica, was up to 16 inches (40 centimetres) in length, and had a triangular broad skull with enormous pear-shaped eye orbits. It also possessed sizeable nostrils and a large centrally placed opening in the skull roof - the pineal foramen, supposedly associated with a light-sensitive glandular structure, the pineal organ, which is a feature of many reptilian groups. The back of the skull was equipped with short spikes, whose function is uncertain. The jaws were powerfully built, and the broad teeth were evidently used for crushing tough plant food.

Possible relatives of the procolophonids are the much larger pareiasaurs of the Late Permian, such as Scutosaurus from the western USSR. Pareiasaurs were bulky animals, up to 10 feet (three metres) in length and built like bomb shelters, with elephantine limbs and skin armored throughout with small nodules of bone. The skull is triangular and bears horns, as in the procolophonids, and the teeth and jaw shapes suggest a diet of rough vegetation. The massive proportions of the pareiasaurs may have been some protection against predation by the gorgonopsians.

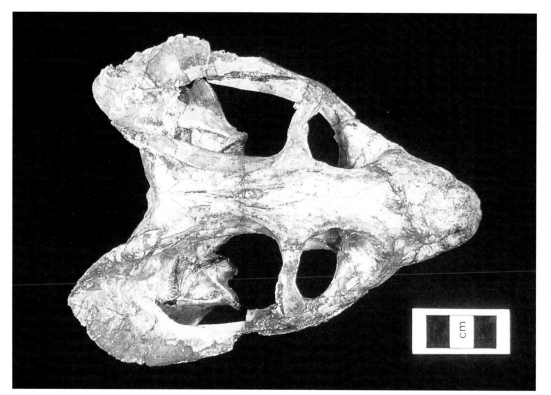

Dorsal (top) view of the skull of the dicynodont Dicynodon *(left, one of the most common reptiles of the South African Karroo Basin. This view shows the small eye sockets and the great breadth of the back of the skull. The broad jugal flanges are very clear, sweeping out to each side around the large temporal openings.*

PERMIAN DIAPSID REPTILES

The final minor group of Permian reptiles were the diapsids. Although diapsids were later to rule the Earth, and gave rise to such successful groups as the birds and the lizards and snakes, they very much held second stage during the Permian - a period of domination by the synapsids. The diapsids actually seem to have been marginalised and able to exploit only a few odd ecological niches that the synapsids had not themselves occupied. Thus, there was a variety of aquatic diapsids in the Late Permian, as well as some gliding forms that were the first flying vertebrates. Insects had conquered the air 100 million years earlier, probably in the Late Devonian, but vertebrates were very slow to follow.

The weigeltisaurs, like *Coelurosauravus* from Madagascar, looked roughly lizard-like in bodily proportions, but they had an extraordinary expanded wing on each side made from skin supported on elongated ribs. When stationary, *Coelurosauravus* could fold its wings back along its sides to keep them out of the way. If it wanted to leap from one tree to another, or down to the ground, it spread out the wings and parachuted gently for many tens of yards before coming in to land. Several modern lizards have independently evolved this ability, as did some other fossil groups (see Chapter 4).

Robert Broom (1866-1951), one of the key figures in establishing the wealth of the fossil reptiles of southern Africa above). Broom was an austere but brilliant Scot who trained as a medical doctor. He worked first in Australia before moving to South Africa in about 1900. He named dozens of new species of therapsids.

A less dramatic, but more typical, diapsid was the younginiform *Youngina* from South Africa. In general anatomy it was not much different from its distant ancestor *Petrolacosaurus* from the Late Carboniferous, but it had larger temporal fenestrae, a shorter neck, and several specifically-lizard-like characters.

Some close relatives of *Youngina*, the hovasaurids such as *Hovasaurus* (from the Late Permian of Madagascar) became adapted to an aquatic lifestyle. These animals could still have moved around on land, with their broadly lizard-like bodies and limbs. But the tail was much modified for swimming, being longer than the rest of the body, and bearing deep fins above and below. Many specimens of *Hovasaurus* have also been found with stomach stones lying within the area of the rib cage. These were probably used as ballast, in order to allow the animal to dive, just as they are in crocodilians today.

MASS EXTINCTION AT THE END
OF THE PERMIAN

The diverse and abundant animal communities of the Late Permian came to a seemingly abrupt end about 245 million years ago. It is hard to be sure just when the great dyings began, and how long they took, because of problems in comparing the ages of rock formations from Europe, Asia, southern Africa, and South America. Needless to say, of some 37 families of tetrapods present in the last five million years of the Permian, 27 rapidly died out. They included numerous amphibians, the captorhinids and pareiasaurs, possibly the weigeltisaurs and younginiforms, and most of the therapsids (dinocephalians, most dicynodonts, gorgonopsians, and others).

This great dying off, which saw the end of nearly

A typical scene in the Karroo. Vast thicknesses of fossil-rich sandstones and mudstones, deposited in ancient rivers and lakes, are exposed by torrential rain and baking heat in summer. Here, mudstones of the Cistecephalus Zone (Late Permian) are capped by resistant layers of basalt, lava that poured from volcanoes.

three-quarters of land-dwelling vertebrate families, must be counted as a mass extinction. It appears to coincide with a major mass extinction in the sea, when numerous groups of arthropods, shellfish, corals, and other marine animals disappeared. Indeed, the end-Permian event is now recognized as the largest mass extinction of all time, since it saw the end of over one-half of all animal and plant families, and as many as 95% of all species, apparently within a limited amount of time. This event is clearly larger than the more famous mass extinction that wiped out the dinosaurs and the other great reptiles, some 180 million years

continued on page 60

A mounted skeleton of the Russian pareiasaur Scutosaurus, *showing the heavy build of the trunk and limbs, and the relatively small skull. The barrel-like rib cage and abdomen must have accommodated a gargantuan digestive system, and it is likely that the pareiasaurs fed on extremely low-grade vegetation.*

Scientists examine finds in the Karroo in South Africa. This fossil-rich area has yielded up thousands of superb specimens since the turn of the century when Robert Broom began excavations in the area. Broom carried out digs wearing a top hat, tailcoat, and high starched collar.

SCUTOSAURUS

The pareiasaurs were a successful, but short-lived, group. They are known from the Late Permian of southern Africa, South America, and the USSR. Scutosaurus from the U.S.S.R. was a typically bulky herbivore, with heavy sprawling limbs and a spiny skull. The skin was probably covered in bony nodules, too. The purpose of all this spinosity is uncertain, unless it was used to ward off attacks from the predatory gorgonopsians.

HOVASAURUS

The Late Permian was dominated by mammal-like reptiles, but some evolution of diapsids, such as the aquatic Hovasaurus, took place at the same time. Hovasaurus was a small animal, clearly adapted to life in the water because of its long, deep, propulsive tail; but it was also capable of moving on land. It presumably fed on small fishes and invertebrates.

later.

The cause of the extinction is not known. There may have been major changes in air and sea temperatures which seriously disturbed all communities of plants and animals. There may also have been distruptive effects caused by the drifting continents as they came together to form the supercontinent, Pangaea, which was in train at that time. As continents fused, shallow seas were lost, coastal areas became buckled up and transformed into inland zones, and habitat variety was lost on land and in the sea. It has even been suggested that there was a catastrophic impact of an asteroid or a comet shower at the end of the Permian period. However, there is no evidence for such a dramatic event at this time, although some exists for such an impact later on (see page 137).

Whatever the cause, the great extinction of reptile families must have cleared the world of much of its terrestrial animal diversity. It left a strange and eerie landscape, to be recolonised by the small number of surviving species.

The gliding reptile Coelurosauravus *from the Late Permian of Durham, northern England; it is also known from Germany, Madagascar and western Canada. The fossil shows the dark-brown backbone running from left to right, and the long ribs above. These were covered by a membrane of skin in life. The ribs bear joints that allowed them to fold the membrane back when not in use.*

CHAPTER 3

THE RULING REPTILES

The ruling reptiles - the archosaurs - rose to dominance during the Triassic period (245-208 million years ago). They include such key groups as the terrestrial dinosaurs, flying pterosaurs, crocodilians, and ultimately birds. The Triassic period was an important time in the evolution of the reptiles, during which the archosaurs diversified and replaced the mammal-like reptiles ecologically. It was also the time during which the mammals and turtles arose.

THE TRIASSIC SCENE

The Triassic world was similar to that of the Permian in many ways. All continents remained united as the supercontinent Pangaea, and there is strong evidence that land animals could migrate freely over most parts of the world. There is no evidence that particular groups were restricted to individual continents, or even smaller areas, as is the case today. This is one reason why palaeontologists are happy to reconstruct phylogenies - diagrams that chart the relationships between major biological groups – and track the course of major events, by compiling information from all corners of the Triassic world.

Triassic climates appear to have been generally warm,

Collecting fossil reptiles in Triassic rocks of southern Africa. The bones of an archosaur skull have been partially weathered out of the Mid Triassic strata in the Ruhuhu Valley, Tanzania. The conditions of burial, and more recent erosion, have broken up the bones. They have to be excavated carefully by hand, using small chisels and brushes. The pieces will then be cleaned and repaired in the laboratory to provide a nearly complete specimen for study.

with much less variation from the poles to the equator than we have today. This is partly because there were no polar ice caps; temperatures at the poles were above freezing. During the Triassic, there was apparently a broad climatic shift, at least in terms of the reptile-

A typical scene in the Karroo Basin of South Africa: sediments of the Lystrosaurus Zone (Lower Triassic) near Harrismith, Orange Free State.

bearing rock formations, from warm and moist conditions early in the period, to hot and dry by its close. This has been determined by a comparison of sedimentary conditions and climatic indicators associated with reptiles dating from all parts of the Triassic.

Most Early Triassic reptiles seem to have been associated with plants and coal deposits that indicate warm, moist climates. Middle and early Late Triassic reptiles were associated with fewer coals, and more with the indicators of aridity such as fossil calcareous soils and thick beds of gypsum, both of which form only during phases of major drying. Many of the very Late Triassic and Early Jurassic dinosaur remains are found in red beds (sandstones and mudstones of predominantly red color), with associated calcareous soils, salt deposits (gypsum, halite), and dune sandstones. Climatic conditions were hot, subtropical, and arid or semi-arid, with only rare or erratic rainfall. The climatic trends during

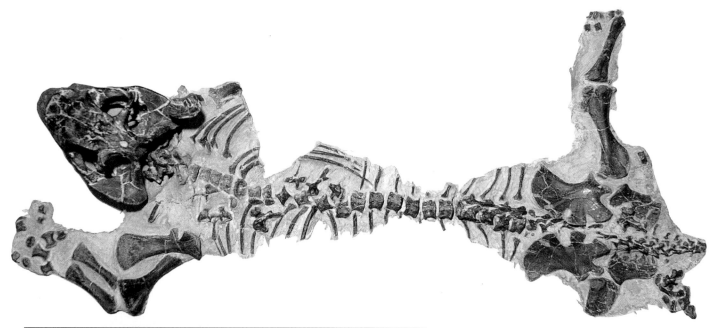

A skeleton of Lystrosaurus *(above), the most common reptile of the Early Triassic. This specimen is displayed roughly as it was found, spread out in the sediments.*

Side view of the skull of Lystrosaurus *(left), showing the short snout, large eye socket and tusk.*

the Triassic may well have had significant effects on reptilian evolution, as we shall see.

TRIASSIC THERAPSIDS

Although the archosaurs were to replace the therapsids as the dominant land animals by the end of the Triassic, these mammal-like reptiles had not been completely decimated by the end-Permian mass extinction. Indeed, they were the first group to recover from the devasta-

tion. The oldest Triassic fossil reptiles consist mainly of mammal-like reptiles, although admittedly in a bizarre and unbalanced way.

The dicynodont *Lystrosaurus*, distantly related to the Late Permian dicynodonts, was the most common reptile on the Earth - to the extent that it formed over 90% of every animal community from South Africa and Antarctica to China, India and the eastern Russia *Lystrosaurus* was a medium-sized animal, no doubt an efficient herbivore, and adapted to a variety of habitats.

ARCHOSAUROMORPHS

The archosaurs and their relatives were a highly successful diapsid group during the Mesozoic Era. This cladogram shows the postulated relationships of the early archosauromorphs (rhynchosaurs, trilophosaurs, prolacertiforms) and the archosaurs themselves (Triassic "thecodontians," crocodilians, pterosaurs, dinosaurs, and birds). The Archosauromorpha arose in the Late Permian. They evolved modestly from then to the Early Triassic, with the mammal-like reptiles still dominant during this time. During the early part of the Triassic, the Archosauria split into two major lines, Crocodylotarsi and Ornithosuchia, both of which included important extinct groups, and both of which survive today - as crocodilians and birds, respectively. This cladogram may be seen in the context of general reptilian evolution on pages 12–13. A more detailed cladogram of the pterosaurs and birds is shown on page 85.

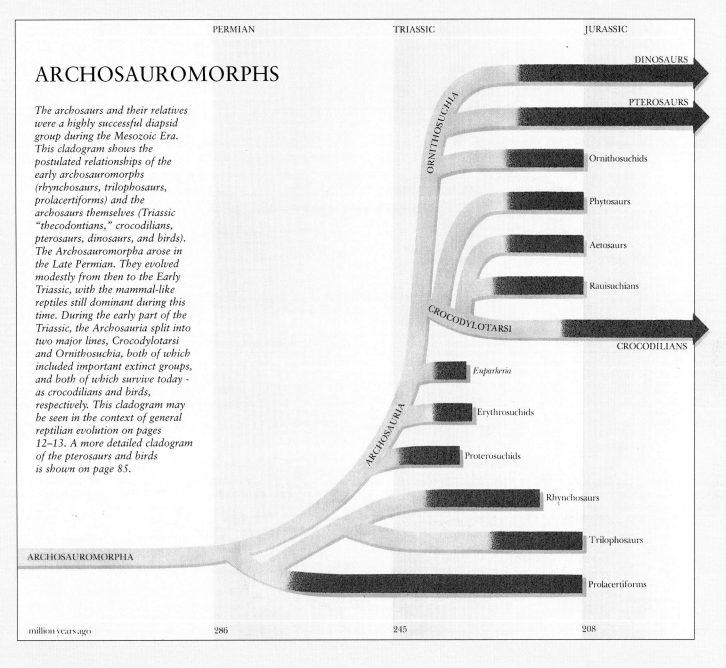

But the only reason for its incredible domination must be that it was able to exploit a world that was empty of similar herbivores.

The dicynodonts radiated (evolved rapidly and diversified) for a second time in the Triassic, and they became moderately varied before they finally died out in the middle of the Late Triassic. Some of the later forms, like *Kannemeyeria* from southern Africa and *Dinodontosaurus* from South America, became large and massively built. Their skulls had high parietal crests along the mid-line, which were probably anchorage areas for massive jaw muscles, and they had vast barrel-

like rib cages to accommodate a long and efficient digestive system, like certain other Late Permian herbivores.

CYNODONTS AND THE LINE TO MAMMALS

The other main therapsid group of the Triassic, and ultimately of greater significance than the dicynodonts, were the cynodonts - descendants of *Procynosuchus*, described previously, from the Late Permian. *Thrinaxodon*, a typical Early Triassic cynodont, was a lightly built carnivore 20 inches (50 centimetres) long,

A large skull of the dicynodont Kannemeyeria *(left), from the Early Triassic of South Africa. Note the high beak, the tusk, the small eye socket, and the flaring jugal bones.*

A skeleton of the large dicynodont Dinodontosaurus *(below) from the Late Triassic of Brazil. The skull is heavy, the body barrel-shaped, and the tail unusually short for a reptile.*

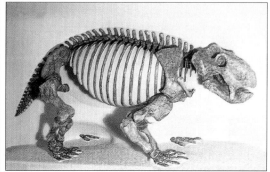

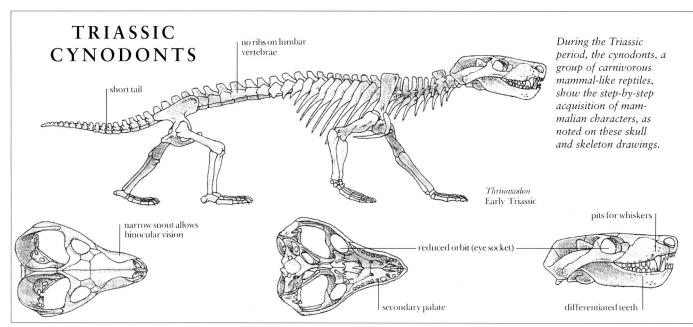

TRIASSIC CYNODONTS

no ribs on lumbar vertebrae

short tail

narrow snout allows binocular vision

Thrinaxodon Early Triassic

reduced orbit (eye socket)

pits for whiskers

secondary palate

differentiated teeth

During the Triassic period, the cynodonts, a group of carnivorous mammal-like reptiles, show the step-by-step acquisition of mammalian characters, as noted on these skull and skeleton drawings.

which may have looked rather like an overweight labrador dog in life. The skull of *Thrinaxodon* shows some major advances toward the mammalian condition. For example, the secondary palate (our hard palate) was nearly complete, with extensive secondary fusion of the maxillae (upper jaws) and the palatine bones in the roof of the mouth. This is a key mammalian character: there is firm separation between the nasal cavity and the mouth, so that mammals (and advanced cynodonts) can chew their food while breathing at the same time. Typical reptiles have to choose

between eating and breathing, since they cannot do both together, a rather inefficient arrangement..

Other mammalian characters of *Thrinaxodon* are seen in the teeth, which match the arrangement of our own. The lower jaw is now made largely from the dentary bone, as in mammals, and the other four bony elements of the reptilian lower jaw are reduced in size and shifted well back. There is also a broad zygomatic arch, the arch of the "cheek bone" beneath our eyes, and the dentary bone runs up inside this arch in *Thrinaxodon*, as it does in mammals.

Advanced features of the rest of the skeleton include a double ball-and-socket joint between the back of the skull and the neck (reptiles have a single ball-and-socket). The vertebrae of the back separate into trunk vertebrae near the head, which are equipped with ribs, and lumbar vertebrae behind, which are not - another mammalian feature not seen in reptiles. The tail is short, and the limbs have become modified from the primitive pattern. The hindlimbs, in particular, have swung inward, and they operate almost in an upright or erect manner. When walking, *Thrinaxodon* swung its legs back and forth in line with the backbone, just as in modern mammals; earlier therapsids, and other reptiles, adopted a sprawling posture and swung their legs in a sweeping motion, sideways and backward and forward. The erect posture is more efficient in terms of speed and

dogs today. Whiskers are of course modified hairs, and the presence of whiskers in *Thrinaxodon* would mean that its whole body must have been covered with hair. This in turn would mean that *Thrinaxodon*, and later cynodonts at least, were fully endothermic - that is, they controlled their body temperatures by internal means, just as mammals do, using the hair for insulation.

Later Triassic cynodonts include the herbivorous diademodonts, such as *Massetognathus*, which had broad skulls with narrow snouts. The cheek teeth were a particular feature, being generally like our own molars. For the first time, cynodonts had broad cheek teeth with complex patterns of cusps (lumps) and depressions, that matched the cusps of the molars in the opposite jaw when the mouth closed, and interlocked (occluded) in a very precise way. Occlusion of the cheek

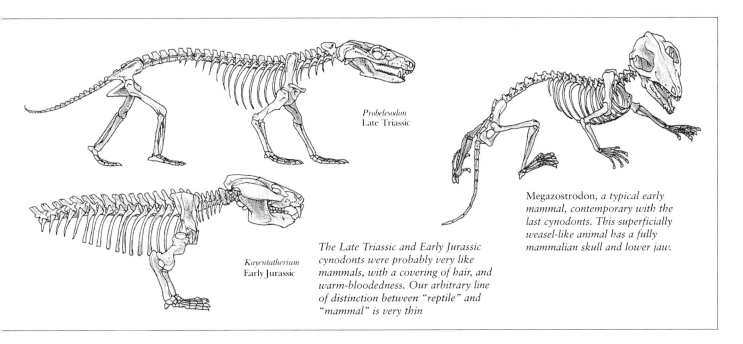

Probelesodon
Late Triassic

Kayentatherium
Early Jurassic

The Late Triassic and Early Jurassic cynodonts were probably very like mammals, with a covering of hair, and warm-bloodedness. Our arbitrary line of distinction between "reptile" and "mammal" is very thin

Megazostrodon, *a typical early mammal, contemporary with the last cynodonts. This superficially weasel-like animal has a fully mammalian skull and lower jaw.*

endurance, and it solves many problems of weight support. Oddly enough, the evolutionary shift to an erect gait in the therapsid line took place at the same time as in the archosaurs, but it was clearly quite independent (as explained below).

Thrinaxodon is often restored and reconstructed as an animal with hair. Strange as it may seem, there is fairly strong fossil evidence for this. In the snout region of the skull, small canals in the bone indicate the presence of blood vessels and nerves that possibly passed through the bone to supply sensory whiskers, just as in cats and

teeth is an essential prerequisite for efficient chewing, a specifically mammalian adaptation, and the herbivorous cynodonts were the first creatures the beginnings of this mammalian ability.

REPTILE OR MAMMAL?

Some advanced carnivorous cynodonts, such as the Late Triassic chiniquodontid *Probelesodon* from Brazil, were small and highly active predators. The limbs were slender, and the skull very mammalian in appearance. A second herbivorous group, the tritylodonts, spanned from the Late Triassic to the Middle Jurassic, well after the extinction of all other therapsids. The tritylodonts seem to have been like reptilian rodents, armed with enlarged gnawing incisors and a battery of broad, grinding cheek teeth. The lower jaw was deep, indicating the presence of powerful jaw muscles, and feeding activities included highly efficient chewing.

The tritylodonts are so close to being true mammals that it has proved hard to draw the line between reptile and mammal. The anatomical changes required to cross the boundary are so small as to appear trifling; they are merely a few minor switches in the function of the small bones at the back of the lower jaw. The oldest mammalian teeth have been dated as Late Triassic, and the first reasonably complete mammals are known from the Early Jurassic. One example, *Morganucodon*, probably looked rather like a scruffy weasel, about 4 inches (10 centimetres) long, with a slender body and short limbs. It was an active insectivore. Mammals evolved in a variety of directions during the rest of the Jurassic and the Cretaceous, but they were unable to achieve a size larger than that of a domestic cat until the dinosaurs died out 65 million years ago. Thus, the mammals arose in the Late Triassic, but they had to wait in the wings for 150 million years or so, until the dinosaurs had disappeared.

In summary, the therapsids went through various major evolutionary advances during the Triassic, but they did not by any means dominate animal life. A variety of non-therapsid reptiles came and went during this time period.

DIVERSE DIAPSIDS OF THE TRIASSIC

The most important diapsid reptiles in the Triassic were of course the archosaurs. But some of their close relatives, including the trilophosaurs, prolacertiforms, and rhynchosaurs, were important in certain fossil faunas.

The trilophosaurs have proved to be by far the most enigmatic group. Although they show all the other characters of the archosaur branch of the diapsids, they actually have only one temporal fenestra on each side of the skull! It has to be assumed that the other one was lost secondarily. *Trilophosaurus*, from the Late Triassic of Texas, has a high-sided heavy skull, a beak-like snout, and unusual broad, flattened teeth that were used for shearing through tough plant food.

The prolacertiforms were moderate-sized animals that probably looked like long-necked lizards in life. They included the spectacular *Tanystropheus*, a partially marine animal described on pages 115-116.

Possible close relatives of the trilophosaurs were the rhynchosaurs, known especially from the Middle and early Late Triassic. They occurred nearly worldwide and were always numerically dominant, representing between two- and three-fifths of all fossil skeletons found in their communities. A typical Late Triassic form, *Hyperodapedon* from Scotland and India, had a high-sided skull that is triangular in plan view. Indeed,

Skeleton of the curios reptile Trilophosaurus, *from the Late Triassic Dockum Formation of Texas. This reptile has been moved around the phylogenetic tree many times since its discovery in the 1940s. It presently resides in the archosauromorph branch of the diapsids, close to the rhynchosaurs. The problem is that* Trilophosaurus *has only one temporal opening, and yet all its other features show it to be a diapsid - the group characterized by two temporal openings! The shape of the skeleton, and in particular the limbs, is very like a large lizard; yet the skull is heavy and solid. The broad cheek teeth indicate a tough plant diet.*

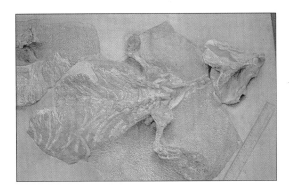

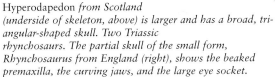
Hyperodapedon *from Scotland*
(underside of skeleton, above) is larger and has a broad, tri-
angular-shaped skull. Two Triassic
rhynchosaurs. The partial skull of the small form,
Rhynchosaurus *from England (right), shows the beaked*
premaxilla, the curving jaws, and the large eye socket.

these later rhynchosaurs had skulls that were considerably wider at the back than they were long, a very unusual feature for a reptile. It indicates the presence of extremely powerful jaw-closing muscles. But for the rhynchosaurs, their teeth are the key to their success.

THE FEEDING HABITS OF RHYNCHOSAURS

The lower jaw of a typical rhynchosaur bears a tightly packed row of peg-shaped teeth along its upper knife-like edge, and a second row slightly below the top, on the inside face of the jaw. The lower jaw teeth cut upward into a V-shaped groove in a broad tooth-plate borne on the maxilla in the upper jaw. Seen from below, the tooth-plate is triangular in shape, being broadest at the back, and it bears three or four longitudinal rows of teeth on each side of the midline groove. The individual teeth of both jaws are deeply rooted and firmly fused into the bone, and their tips are pointed when they erupt (grow out of the gum), but they soon become worn flat in line with the surrounding bone. This remarkable dentition has provoked much debate as to its function.

One suggestion was that the rhynchosaurs fed on fresh-water clams. They scraped them out of rivers and lakes with tusk-like premaxilla bones at the front of the mouth, and crushed them with their great slabs of maxillary teeth. Indeed, such clams have been found preserved in the sediments, along with one or two rhynchosaur species. However, when it is examined more closely, the rhynchosaur dentition is not adapted for

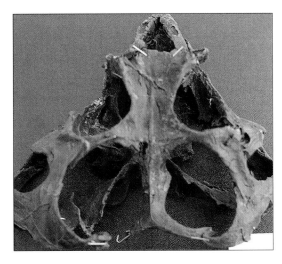
This vinyl cast of its skull (above) shows the single nostril, the eye sockets, and the large temporal openings.

such crushing activity. Bear in mind that the lower jaw has a knife-like cutting edge, not a pounding board to match the upper tooth-plate, as is the case in animals that eat hard-shelled molluscs (see placodonts, pages 118–120). The rhynchosaur closed its jaws with a firm shearing motion, rather like a pair of scissors. There was no back-and-forth, sideways, or rotating motion. This is shown by two separate pieces of evidence: the jaw joint is a very precise rocker-and-socket arrange-

The ghostly hand of the small rhynchosaur Rhynchosaurus articeps, *a specimen from Grinshill Quarry, Shropshire, in the English Midlands. This was the first rhynchosaur to be described, in 1841. The hand is delicately preserved in the form of the original bone, virtually unaltered, embedded in a fine-grained, buff-coloured sandstone that was deposited by a gently flowing river in warm, rather monsoonal, conditions.* Rhynchosaurus *had five fingers, just as we do, and lizard-like proportions.*

ment that prevents any sliding or rotation; and precise wear pits can be found in rhynchosaur specimens where a tooth has created a matching depression in the opposite jaw.

Rhynchosaurs probably fed on tough vegetation which they dug up with their powerful scratching hind feet, raked together with the premaxillary "tusks," and pulled into their mouths with a muscular tongue. The stems and leaves were cut up by precise scissor-like shearing actions of the jaws. The sharp, unworn teeth at the edges of the maxillary tooth plate, that did not interlock with the opposite jaw, served to hold the plant material in place while it was being cut up. Additional evidence for herbivory are the vast barrel-like rib cage of the rhynchosaurs and the great abundance of the species. It is well known in ecology that herbivores, the animals at the bottom of food chains, are nearly always present in much greater numbers than carnivores.

The first rhynchosaur to be described, *Rhynchosaurus articeps* from the Middle Triassic of England, was named by Sir Richard Owen in 1841. To begin with, he interpreted the bones as those of an amphibian, but soon came to regard it as a lizard. Bain's discovery of *Dicynodon* (page 54) confused matters, since Owen for a while thought that rhynchosaurs and dicynodonts were related on the basis of the paired "tusks" in both forms. This was a false comparison, since the "tusks" of the dicynodonts were the usual canine teeth, but those of rhynchosaurs were the premaxillary bones and not true tusks at all. Later, Owen and others made a link between the Triassic rhynchosaurs and the living tuatara, *Sphenodon*, a famous lizard-like "living fossil" that had just been reported from New Zealand at the time. Palaeontologists accepted this interpretation until about 1980, when a variety of evidence showed that the rhynchosaurs had much more in common with the archosaurs than with the lizards and their kin.

MORE TRIASSIC DIAPSID REPTILES

The other branch of the diapsids, the lepidosauromorphs, continued at a low key during the Triassic, having arisen from *Youngina* and its allies of the Late Permian. The lepidosauromorphs would give rise to true lizards in the Late Jurassic, and to snakes in the Early Cretaceous.

The main Late Triassic lepidosauromorphs were the

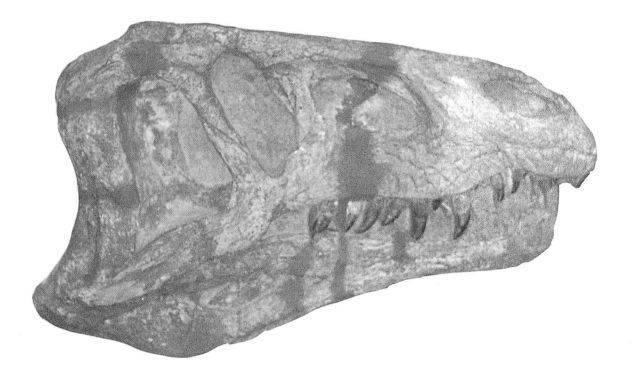

The powerfully built skull of the carnivorous Erythrosuchus, *from the Early Triassic of eastern Cape Province, South Africa. The skull is narrow and deep, and there are a small number of ferocious-looking teeth. These teeth are typical of nearly all archosaurian predators, from these Early Triassic "theodontians" to the Late Cretaceous dinosaur* Tyrannosaurus rex: *they are flattened in cross-section, recurved, and bear sharp serrated edges along front and back.*

sphenodontians, distant ancestors of the living tuatara, mentioned above. A typical early form was *Planocephalosaurus* from the south-west of England. This six-inch (15-centimeter) animal had a blunt snout and rows of short teeth fused to the bones of the jaw, which may have been used to eat plants or insects. Fossil skeletons of *Planocephalosaurus* were found in ancient fissure deposits in Carboniferous limestones around Bristol in southwestern England. During the Triassic, these older limestones were exposed at the surface, and caves and fissures were formed by the dissolving effects of rain. Small animals fell in and were eventually entombed in Late Triassic and Early Jurassic sediments, which preserved their remains - often in exquisite detail. Associated animals include early·dinosaurs, the flying *Kuehneosaurus* (page 84), and pterosaurs.

THE EARLY ARCHOSAURS

The key group of reptiles in the Triassic was undoubtedly the archosaurs, the 'ruling reptiles'. The oldest-known archosaur is actually Permian, but very late Permian, and is represented by only a few fragmentary bones from the former U.S.S.R. The group really became established during the Triassic. The major archosaur groups arose later in the Triassic -the croco-

dilians, dinosaurs, and pterosaurs. Earlier forms, including their ancestors, are generally known informally as 'thecodontians'.

Most of the Triassic archosaurs were carnivores, and they exploited ways of life left vacant in the Early Triassic by the extinction of most therapsid carnivores (dinocephalians, gorgonopsians, and other smaller forms). Bear in mind that the cynodonts were already highly successful and advanced carnivores throughout the Triassic, so the thecodontians were clearly not overwhelmingly successful; they did best as 'crocodile-like'-fish-eaters and giant top carnivores.

The first archosaurs, proterosuchids like *Proterosuchus* from the Early Triassic of South Africa, were long-snouted animals of modest size, about five feet (one and a half metres) long. *Proterosuchus* probably fed on smaller mammal-like reptiles and procolophonids, as well as on freshwater fish, but its short, sprawling limbs meant that it was probably only

continued on page 74

THE DINOSAURS

The dinosaurs are the best-known of fossil reptiles because of their popular appeal. Of course, they are by no means the only fossil reptiles known, nor indeed are they necessarily the most spectacular - as this book attempts to show.

The dinosaurs arose from "thecodontian" archosaurs like *Ornithosuchus* (see page 81), and they are closely related to the pterosaurs (see Chapter 4). The dinosaurs in turn gave rise to the birds.The Dinosauria fall naturally into two subgroups, the Saurischia and the Ornithischia, which may be distinguished by the overall layout of their hip bones, when viewed from the side. Saurischians follow the standard reptilian plan in having a "three-rayed" pelvis, with the pubis pointing forward. In ornithischians, the pubis points backward, parallel to the ischium.

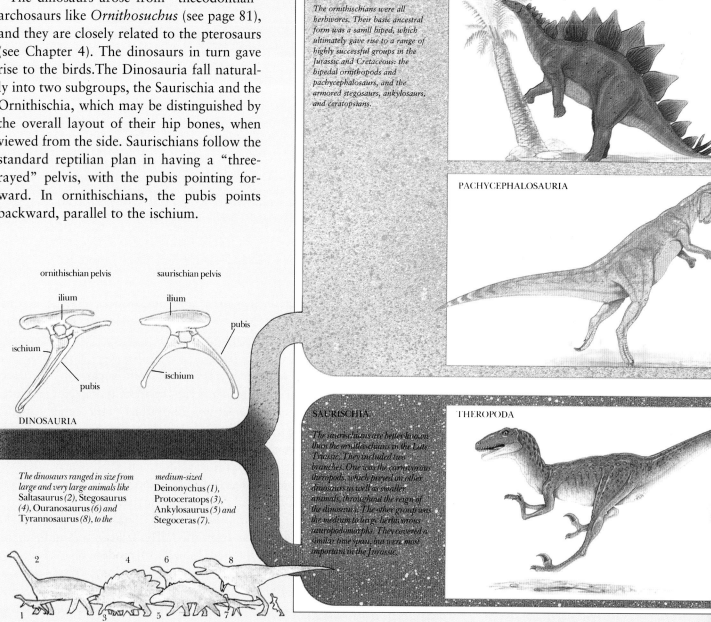

ornithischian pelvis

ilium

ischium

pubis

saurischian pelvis

ilium

pubis

ischium

DINOSAURIA

The dinosaurs ranged in size from large and very large animals like Saltasaurus *(2),* Stegosaurus *(4),* Ouranosaurus *(6) and* Tyrannosaurus *(8), to the*

medium-sized Deinonychus *(1),* Protoceratops *(3),* Ankylosaurus *(5) and* Stegoceras *(7).*

ORNITHISCHIA

The ornithischians were all herbivores. Their basic ancestral form was a samll biped, which ultimately gave rise to a range of highly successful groups in the Jurassic and Cretaceous: the bipedal ornithopods and pachycephalosaurs, and the armored stegosaurs, ankylosaurs, and ceratopsians.

STEGOSAURIA

PACHYCEPHALOSAURIA

SAURISCHIA

The saurischians are better known than the ornithischians in the Late Triassic. They included two branches. One was the carnivorous theropods, which preyed on other dinosaurs as well as smaller animals, throughout the reign of the dinosaurs. The other group was the medium to large herbivorous sauropodomorphs. They covered a similar time span, but were most important in the Jurassic.

THEROPODA

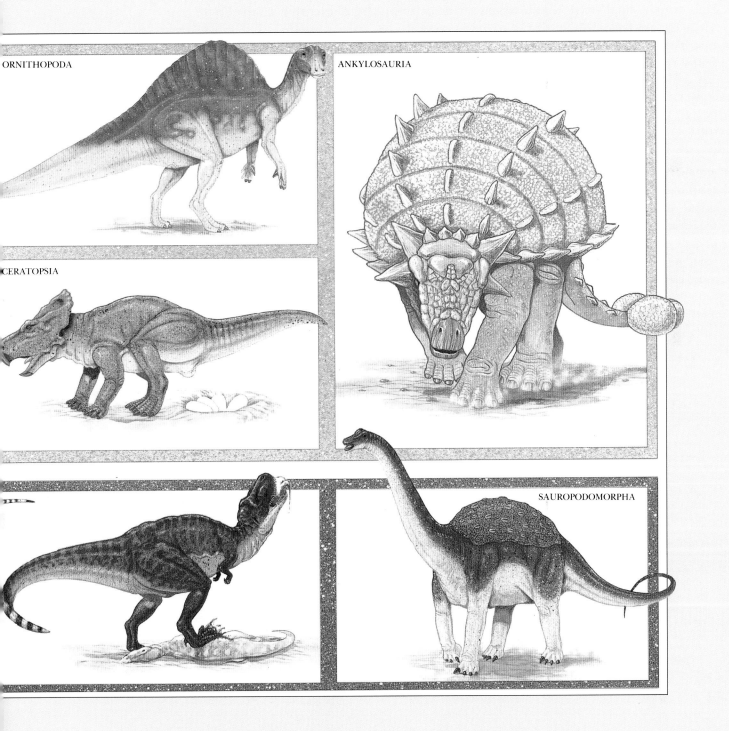

ORNITHOPODA

ANKYLOSAURIA

CERATOPSIA

SAUROPODOMORPHA

capable of short dashes after a particularly tasty prey animal. Its normal mode of progression was doubtless a leisurely waddle.

Proterosuchus shows several key features in the skull and skeleton that are regarded as archosaur hallmarks. There is a special opening in the side of the skull between the nostril and the orbit (eye socket), called the antorbital fenestra. It may have housed a gland of some kind or may simply have been a weight-saving device. The teeth are flat-sided, instead of round in cross section. There is an extra knob-like muscle attachment, the fourth trochanter, on the femur (thigh bone).

A second Early Triassic archosaur group, the erythrosuchids, shows several major advances over the protero-suchids. They were the first large predators of the Triassic. *Vjushkovia* from the U.S.S.R., for example, was 10 feet (three metres) long, and could feed on any animal it came across. *Vjushkovia* had a higher, shorter skull than the proterosuchids. It also showed an additional archosaurian character, the lateral mandibular fenestra, which is an additional opening in the posterior half of the lower jaw. The important advances are seen, however, in the limbs. The pelvis (hip bone) is more clearly three-rayed than in *Proterosuchus*, and the limb bones are relatively longer, both features contributing to movement.

The most advanced thecodontian of the Early Triassic is a much smaller animal called *Euparkeria*, only 20 inches (50 centimeters) long, from South Africa. This small, active carnivore may have been capable of walking on all fours like a tetrapod – but also running on its hind limbs. If this is true, then *Euparkeria* was the first biped ever to walk the Earth.

ARCHOSAUR ANKLES AND POSTURES

The archosaurs split into two major lineages after the Early Triassic. One, the crocodylotarsans, led ultimately to the crocodiles. The other, ornithosuchians, gave rise to the pterosaurs, dinosaurs, and birds. The key to the split resides in some seemingly minor fiddling with the structure of archosaur ankles.

Proterosuchus, *Vjushkovia*, and *Euparkeria* had the basic archosaur ankle, rather like that of the rhynchosaurs and prolacertiforms, which acted as a simple hinge. In the crocodylotarsans the two main ankle bones, the astragalus and calcaneum (which form the heel in our feet), became capable of rotating against

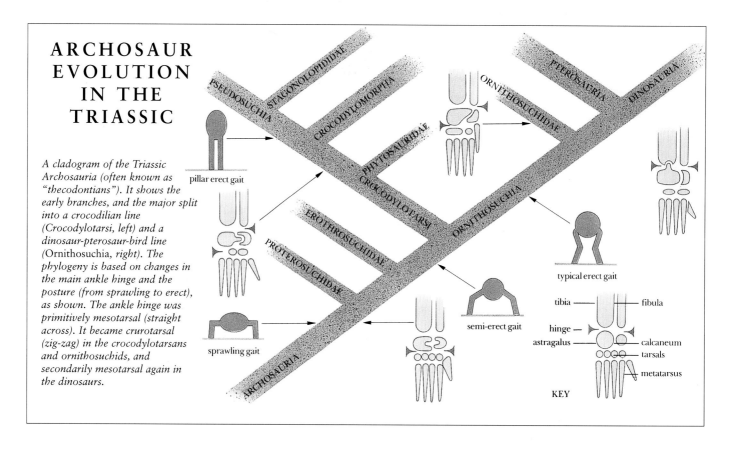

ARCHOSAUR EVOLUTION IN THE TRIASSIC

A cladogram of the Triassic Archosauria (often known as "thecodontians"). It shows the early branches, and the major split into a crocodilian line (Crocodylotarsi, left) and a dinosaur-pterosaur-bird line (Ornithosuchia, right). The phylogeny is based on changes in the main ankle hinge and the posture (from sprawling to erect), as shown. The ankle hinge was primitively mesotarsal (straight across). It became crurotarsal (zig-zag) in the crocodylotarsans and ornithosuchids, and secondarily mesotarsal again in the dinosaurs.

pillar erect gait

sprawling gait

PSEUDOSUCHIA
STAGONOLEPIDIDAE
CROCODYLOMORPHA
PHYTOSAURIDAE
CROCODYLOTARSI
EROTHROSUCHIDAE
PROTEROSUCHIDAE
ARCHOSAURIA
ORNITHOSUCHIDAE
ORNITHOSUCHIA
PTEROSAURIA
DINOSAURIA

semi-erect gait

typical erect gait

tibia — fibula
hinge —
astragalus — calcaneum
— tarsals
— metatarsus

KEY

each other by means of a peg-and-socket-joint. This meant the line of the ankle hinge ran in a stepped path, rather than in a straight line from side to side. The ornithosuchians had two ankle structures, one which was the reverse of the crocodilian arrangement, and one (in pterosaurs, dinosaurs, and birds), which was a new and simplified version with a straight-line hinge.

The modifications to archosaurian ankles were not mere evolutionary tinkering. They were intimately associated with major biomechanical changes in modes of travel that were underway during the Triassic. Most living reptiles, and most reptiles that existed before the Early Triassic, adopt a sprawling posture and mode of locomotion: the knees and elbows stick out sideways, and the humerus and femur (upper arm and leg bones) swing in a roughly horizontal plane during a stride. *Euparkeria*, and later archosaurs, adopted a semi-erect or fully erect posture, in which the limbs moved partially or completely beneath the body. Parallel changes were occurring in the evolution of the cynodonts (page 67). By the end of the Triassic, most reptiles (except for turtles and the ancestors of lizards) had a fully erect posture.

DIVERSITY OF THE CROCODYLOTARSANS

The most primitive crocodylotarsans are the phytosaurs, so far known only from the Late Triassic, but they must have arisen earlier. They are known in abundance from Germany, where they were found as long ago as the 1820s, and from North America as well as Asia and Africa. An Indian phytosaur, *Parasuchus*, shows all of the key features: a long snout armed with numerous short conical teeth, a generally crocodile-like body, and short limbs. *Parasuchus* used its long jaws to seize freshwater fish and small tetrapods. Stomach contents of two specimens include the bones of prolacertiforms and a small rhynchosaur. The nostrils of *Parasuchus* were placed just in front of the eyes, well back from the tip of the snout, and elevated on a low mound of bone. It may be that this arrangement allowed the phytosaur to lurk just beneath the surface of the water, with only the nostrils and eyes showing, while it waited for prey to approach. Crocodilians today adopt the same tactics, although their nostril mound is at the front of the snout.

The true crocodilians arose in the Late Triassic, although these early animals do not look much like our modern crocodiles. For example, *Terrestrisuchus*, a 20-

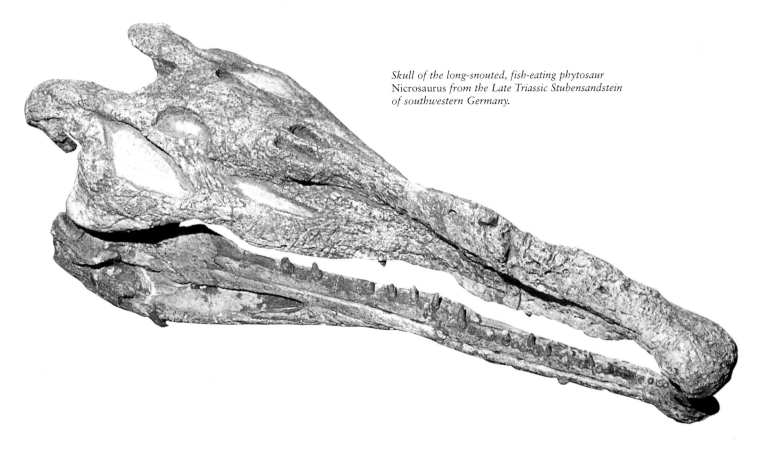

Skull of the long-snouted, fish-eating phytosaur Nicrosaurus *from the Late Triassic Stubensandstein of southwestern Germany.*

PARASUCHUS

The Indian phytosaur Parasuchus is well known from a number of nearly complete skeletons. It looked, and probably behaved, like a typical fresh-water crocodilian, preying on fish and also on small and medium-sized animals at the waterside. But the phytosaurs and crocodilians evolved their peculiar features independently, as shown by a detailed study of their apparently shared characters.
For example, the long, narrow snout of phytosaurs is made from the premaxillae bones, while in crocodilians it is formed from the maxillae.

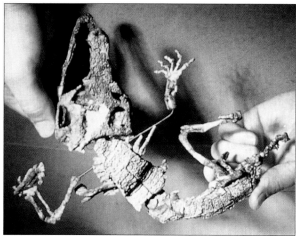

The skeleton of a tiny early crocodilian, Lesothosuchus (left), from the Early Jurassic of Lesotho, southern Africa. The skull roof is roughly square, and the snout is narrow. There are heavy armor plates over much of the trunk and tail. Lesothosuchus was a fast-moving, erect-gaited terrestrial animal, with some aquatic features.

inch (50-centimeter) long animal from South Wales, was a lightly built insectivorous biped. How can this animal be regarded as a crocodilian and not, for example, an early dinosaur? First, it has a crocodylotarsan ankle, so it cannot be placed in the ornithosuchian group. Second, it has several diagnostic crocodilian characters, including long rod-like wrist bones, and a recessed lower temporal fenestra in which the bones at the back of the skull have grown inward to meet the braincase. It was only in Jurassic times that the croco-

dilians became more thoroughly aquatic, mostly in fresh water, but a few in the sea (page 128). The group was relatively successful during the rest of the age of the dinosaurs, but has dwindled since then, with only some 12 species alive today.

THE IMPORTANCE OF HIP JOINTS

The remaining crocodylotarsans of the Triassic include a group of herbivores, the aetosaurs, and a group of carnivores, the rauisuchians. Both of these groups had gone a step further than the phytosaurs and most crocodilians in their postural evolution. They had a fully erect gait, but of a rather unusual type, and quite different from that seen in the ornithosuchians (pterosaurs, dinosaurs, and birds) or in the cynodonts and the line to mammals. In the latter cases, the femur has a ball-like end that projects on a short neck at a right angle to the shaft of the bone – just as in humans.

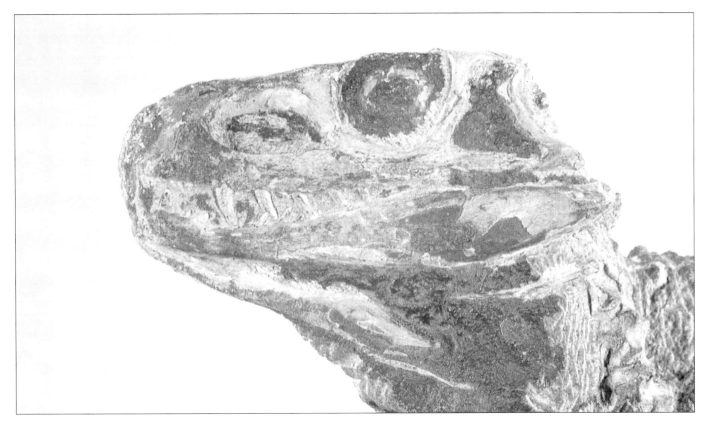

Side view of the skull of Euparkeria, an important early "thecodontian" from the Early Triassic of South Africa. Euparkeria was a lightly built animal, probably capable of walking on two legs. In this, and other features, it is a key precursor of the dinosaurs. The skull is open, and there are a small number of sharp teeth.

The ball fits into a socket in the pelvic bones.

In the aetosaurs and rauisuchians, the femur does not have a ball joint at a right-angle to its shaft. The top of the shaft of the femur fits up into a nearly horizontal socket formed beneath the pelvis. In other words, the pelvic bones have tipped over, and the erect gait is achieved in a pillar-like way in which the whole hindlimb is placed beneath the body, like a column supporting a building. The more familiar erect posture of birds, mammals, dinosaurs, and pterosaurs is "buttress-like:" the architectural analogy is used more appropriately with the buttress of a building, which supports it from the side, rather than with a column.

The aetosaurs were the first herbivorous archosaurs, a successful group and known worldwide, but restricted to the Late Triassic. Stagonolepis, from Scotland, was up to 10 feet (three metres) long, and had a broadly crocodile-like armoured body, short limbs, a heavy tail, and a strangely small head. The skull had a blunt, upturned snout that may have been used as a small shovel to dig around in the soil for edible tubers and roots, which were then cut up by the rather weak, peg-like teeth. The body was encased in an armour of heavy bony plates set into the skin – a defence against the major predators of the time, the rauisuchians.

The rauisuchians were a diverse group known from the fossilised remains of 20 or more Middle and Late Triassic species. An advanced form, Saurosuchus from the Late Triassic of Brazil, reached 23 feet (seven metres) in length, and was clearly capable of eating the largest aetosaurs, rhynchosaurs, and dicynodonts with ease. Saurosuchus had a high-sided skull and jaws armed with dagger-like teeth, a short neck and long limbs held in a pillar-erect posture that enabled it to move with speed. Rauisuchian footprints, known as Cheirotherium, have been found in many parts of the world, and they demonstrate their advanced gait.

In the past, many rauisuchian remains have been confused with those of large carnivorous dinosaurs. Their teeth, for example, are virtually indistinguishable from those of the Late Cretaceous dinosaur *Tyrannosaurus*. However, there is clearly no direct relationship with the rauisuchians, as some palaeontologists have suggested, because of fundamental differences in their limb structures. The teeth and jaws are superficially similar

continued on page 80

REPTILES OF THE LATE TRIASSIC

This scene in southern Brazil, some 230 million years ago, represents the Santa Maria Formation and shows a fauna that was typical of most parts of the world at that time. The most common animals were the herbivorous rhynchosaurs, *Scaphonyx* (mid-left). Other herbivores included the small cynodont mammal-like reptile, *Traversodon* (bottom left), and the giant dicyndont, *Dinodontosaurus* (deceased, right).

The predators were varied in both relationships and adaptations. The largest were the rauisuchian thecodontians, such as *Rauisuchus* (top left). Smaller examples were the cynodonts Belesodon (bottom right) and the bipedal archosaur *Staurikosaurus* (top left) – possibly the oldest known dinosaur in the world.

The world as it was then

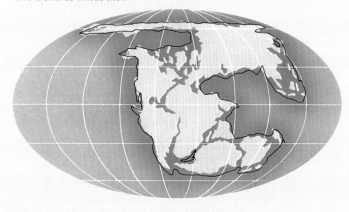

Size ranges in the Late Triassic were similar to those in the Late Permian. The giant was the dicynodont Dinodontosaurus (1), and midgets were the cynodonts Belesodon (2) and Traversodon (3). Larger carnivores included the thecodontian Rauisuchus (4) and the early dinosaur Staurikosaurus (5), while the most common animal was the rhynchosaur Scaphonyx (6).

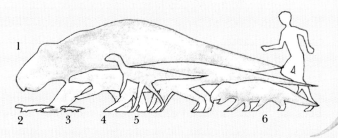

because they represent the best set of adaptations for successful predation, but they have evolved independently.

THE ORIGIN OF THE DINOSAURS AND PTEROSAURS

The second key archosaur lineage, evolving in parallel with the crocodylotarsans just described, was the ornithosuchia. The typical ornithosuchians are the ornithosuchids such as *Ornithosuchus*, 10 feet (three metres) long and from the Late Triassic of Scotland. (Note that the names "ornithosuchian" and "ornithosuchid" indicate quite different groups of animals. The latter refers to a restricted Late Triassic family, and the former to the large group including the ornithosuchids, but also the pterosaurs, dinosaurs, and birds. The similarity of names is bound to cause confusion, but it has arisen from the history of how palaeontologists have developed their knowledge of these animals. Group names cannot be changed at a whim because that might also cause confusion, unfortunately!)

Ornithosuchus is an obvious predator which presumably fed on rhynchosaurs like *Hyperodapedon* and aetosaurs like *Stagonolepis*, which have been found with it. *Ornithosuchus* had the beginnings of the pillar-like erect posture seen in the dinosaurs, and it could probably move about on all fours or bipedally. Its ankle was of a peculiar type, functionally similar to that of the crocodylotarsans, but its structure shows that it evolved independently; it was also different from that of the pterosaurs and dinosaurs.

Pterosaurs and dinosaurs share a simple hinge-like ankle, in which the astragalus and calcaneum (page 74) are fused to the shin bones (the tibia and fibula). The hinge line of the ankle runs straight across, between the astragalus-and-calcaneum unit and the remaining ankle and toe bones. Placing pterosaurs and dinosaurs close together in their evolutionary relationships, and putting both of them in the ornithosuchian branch of archosaurian evolution is still highly controversial; but a number of independent analyses have tended to confirm this view. Previously, pterosaur ancestry had been sought at various positions in the evolutionary tree of the thecodontians, and even completely outside the Archosauria.

The origin of the dinosaurs seemed even more problematic. Many paleontologists thought that there was no such real group as the Dinosauria; there were really two, three, or even four groups, that looked superficially similar, but which had entirely separate origins from different thecodontian families. The new cladistic type of analyses of the Archosauria, produced since 1985, have proved quite revolutionary in sharpening up our views of early archosaur evolution.

TURNOVER IN THE LATE TRIASSIC

The Late Triassic was a time of spectacular change. Many previously important reptile groups died out: the procolophonids, trilophosaurs, rhynchosaurs, prolacertiforms, phytosaurs, aetosaurs, rauisuchians, ornithosuchids, dicynodonts, and most cynodonts. New reptiles appeared: turtles, sphenodontians, crocodilians, pterosaurs, and dinosaurs (as well as mammals). At one time, it was thought that there was some kind of large-scale competitive process under way, in which the thecodontians and rhynchosaurs competed with the mammal-like reptiles and replaced them, and in turn the dinosaurs competed with the rhynchosaurs and thecodontians, and replaced them. However, this kind of view is much too simplistic, and the replacement seems to have involved extinction events.

Footprints from the Middle Triassic of northwestern England, made by a creature called Cheirotherium. *These large, hand-like prints were first found in the 1830s, and the position of the "thumb" on the outside of the track proved to be a puzzle. The "thumb" is actually the outer smallest digit of the back foot, and the print shape is that of a rauisuchian. A small hand print lies in front of each foot.*

There were two mass extinctions during the 20–25 million years of the Late Triassic – one near the beginning, the other at the end. The rhynchosaurs, dicynodonts, and many cynodonts died out in the first event, and the dinosaurs were able to exploit the niches left vacant in a way analogous to the situation at the beginning of the Triassic. At the end of the Triassic, the remaining thecodontians and most therapsids disappeared, and the dinosaurs and other new reptile groups were able to diversity further – on land, in the air, and in the sea.

ORNITHOSUCHUS

An advanced "thecodontian" on the ornithosuchian line, and very close to the origin of the pterosaurs and dinosaurs. Ornithosuchus is known from the Late Triassic of Scotland, where it probably preyed on rhynchosaurs, aetosaurs, and smaller animals.

REPTILES OF
THE AIR

Reptiles evolved the ability to take to the air at least five times: once in the Permian period, three times in the Triassic, and once again in the Jurassic. The early aerial reptiles were gliders, but two major groups were active flyers which flapped their wings and achieved powered flight: the pterosaurs, and those which gave rise to the birds.

THE FIRST FLYERS

The Permian weigeltisaurs are the first known flying reptiles. Although tetrapods had ventured onto the land during Late Devonian times, and flying insects had appeared then as well, it took the vertebrates some 120 million years to begin to exploit the air in the same way. Reptiles had no doubt hunted small and large flying insects during the Carboniferous and Early Permian, but they could only leap short distances from the ground or trees to catch their aerial prey.

Today, a remarkable range of tetrapods has evolved gliding adaptations independently of each other: there are flying frogs with great webs of skin between their toes, several groups of flying lizards with expandable webs of skin along their sides, some snakes with broad flat bodies, and various flying squirrels, flying lemurs, and the like among the mammals. All these animals use expanded areas of skin like a parachute, to slow down the rate at which they fall through the air. They can leap from a high tree and control their descent to another branch or to the ground. Gliding flight of this sort allows them to move rapidly through the trees, escape hunting animals, and capture flying prey in mid-trajectory. Indeed, virtually the only tetrapod groups today that do not include gliding or flying members are the turtles, crocodilians and ungulates – mammalian plant-eaters like cattle, horses, and elephants!

The gliding weigeltisaurs are known from the Late Permian rocks of Europe and Madagascar, where some fairly complete fossil skeletons of these delicate animals have been found. *Coelurosauravus*, a typical example from Madagascar (page 61), had enormously elongated ribs which stuck out sideways forming horizontal 'wings'. The ribs could be folded back when the animal was resting or running about: each rib has an articulation point (joint) close to the side of the body. The ribs were presumably covered with skin, and *Coelurosauravus* could have swooped from tree to tree just as well as any modern gliding lizard.

The weigeltisaurs appear to be primitive diapsids. The skull has two temporal openings, as would be expected,

A late Jurassic pterosaur, Pterodactylus suevicus, *a typical example of this highly successful group of flying reptiles. The skull has long narrow jaws lined with sharp teeth, used for capturing fish, and a bulbous brain case, as in birds. The long neck, short back, and short tail run toward the upper right, while the enormously elongated wing fingers run downward and then fold back on themselves. The preservation of the delicate bones is typically as good as this.*

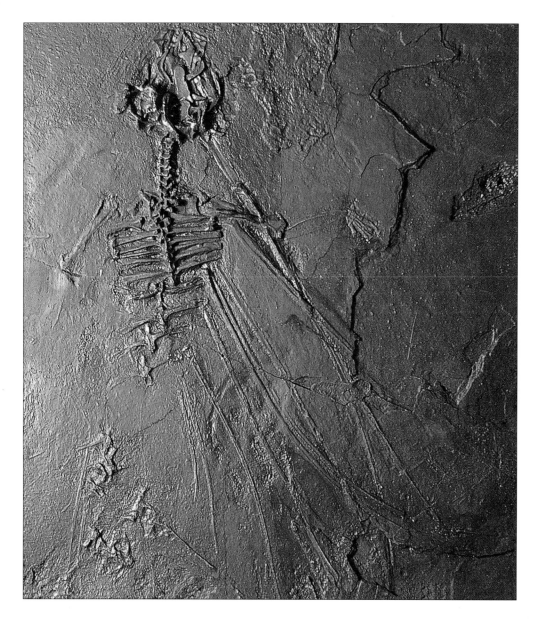

An early gliding reptile, the kuehneosaur Icarosaurus siefkeri, from the Late Triassic of New Jersey. The kuehneosaurs are known from both Europe and the US, where they seem to have been successful, but short-lived. The exquisite preservation of this small skeleton shows the front part nearly intact, with an array of needle-thin ribs running back on the right.

but it shows none of the specialised characters of those early lizards, the lepidosaurs, although at times the weigeltisaurs have been said to be true lizards. The bones at the back of the cheek region of the skull show remarkable 'toothed' margins – a kind of frill – which may have been used as a type of display structure when fighting or mating.

TRIASSIC GLIDERS

Two forms of gliding reptile arose in the Late Triassic. The kuehneosaurs, such as *Icarosaurus* from New York State, and *Kuehneosaurus* from south-western England, were superficially similar to the weigeltisaurs, but they had separate origins. *Kuehneosaurus* is known from

several exquisitely preserved, but rather misshapen, skeletons from the fissures in Carboniferous limestone that yielded the sphenodontian *Planocephalosaurus* and other forms (page 71). The body is lizard-like, and the wings are longer and narrower than those of the weigeltisaurs, each being supported on only ten or so lengthened ribs. The skull of *Kuehneosaurus* is superficially lizard-like, but its group, like the weigeltisaurs, does not seem to show any close affinities with the lepidosaurs.

The second group of Late Triassic gliders is represented by *Longisquama* ('long scale'), possibly an ornithosuchian archosaur, but its relationships are still uncertain. The remarkable fossil skeleton of *Longisquama* was discovered in 1970 in Kirgizstan, Soviet Central

FLYING REPTILES

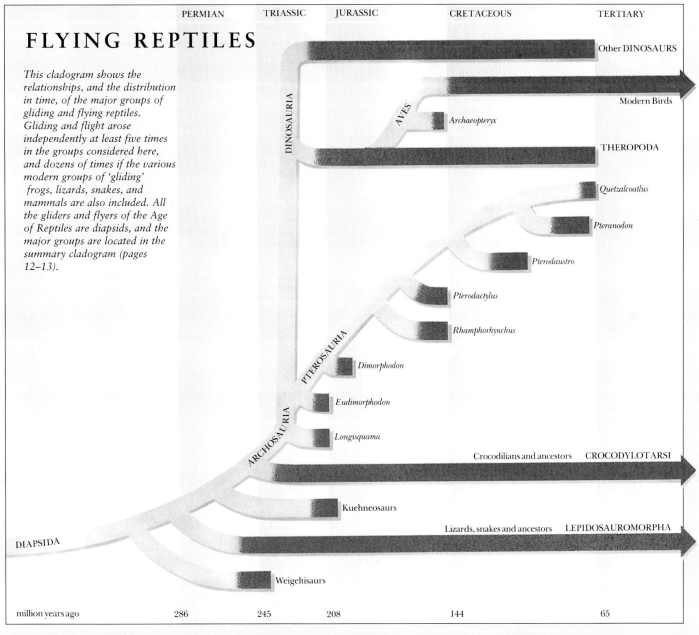

This cladogram shows the relationships, and the distribution in time, of the major groups of gliding and flying reptiles. Gliding and flight arose independently at least five times in the groups considered here, and dozens of times if the various modern groups of 'gliding' frogs, lizards, snakes, and mammals are also included. All the gliders and flyers of the Age of Reptiles are diapsids, and the major groups are located in the summary cladogram (pages 12–13).

PERMIAN TRIASSIC JURASSIC CRETACEOUS TERTIARY

Other DINOSAURS

Modern Birds

Archaeopteryx

AVES

DINOSAURIA

THEROPODA

Quetzalcoatlus

Pteranodon

Pterodaustro

Pterodactylus

Rhamphorhynchus

PTEROSAURIA

Dimorphodon

Eudimorphodon

Longisquama

ARCHOSAURIA

Crocodilians and ancestors CROCODYLOTARSI

Kuehneosaurs

Lizards, snakes and ancestors LEPIDOSAUROMORPHA

DIAPSIDA

Weigeltisaurs

million years ago 286 245 208 144 65

Asia. It shows elongated scales along the backs of the arms and legs, which have been compared to bird feathers. Just as striking is the double row of long strap-like scales along the middle of the back. The preserved specimens seem to stand erect, and they would probably have been in this position when the animal was resting. In flight, however, they probably folded out horizontally and acted as a gliding wing. But the specimen's preservation is not good enough to study the limb or back scale structures in detail, and it is unlikely that *Longisquama* is in any way directly ancestral to birds.

The same Triassic deposits in Kirgizstan produced a second unusual gliding reptile, *Podopteryx* ('foot wing'), which has membranes of skin extending between its hindlimbs, and between its front limbs and the sides of the body. The true affinities of *Podopteryx* are uncertain, but it may be in some way related to the pterosaurs, the first vertebrates with powers of true flight, which also appeared in the Late Triassic.

THE FIRST PTEROSAURS

The pterosaurs arose at about the same time as the dinosaurs, some 230 million years ago, at the beginning of the Late Triassic; they died out in tandem, too, 65 million years ago at the end of the Cretaceous period. In

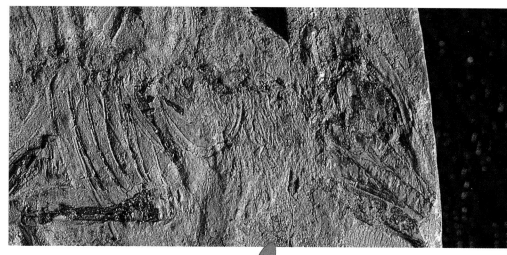

The head of the original fossil specimen of Longisquama (above) from Kirgizstan, Soviet Central Asia. It shows the small, high-domed, vaguely bird-like skull. The small, sharp teeth in the narrow jaws suggest a diet of insects, which Longisquama may have captured while gliding from tree to tree.

LONGISQUAMA

A spectacular reconstruction of a Late Triassic glider. It probably looked like a highly coloured lizard, although in reality Longisquama was more closely related to the dinosaurs and pterosaurs. While resting, the enormously elongated dorsal scales were held erect, as here; but in flight, they were spread out to the side, to provide a broad, gliding wing.

The original specimen of Longisquama, counterpart to the slab on the opposite page, showing how the skeleton and the dorsal scales are preserved as impressions on the orange mudstone.

fact, most palaeontologists now accept that the pterosaurs and dinosaurs share a close common ancestry, and are indeed sister groups (see the cladogram on pages 12–13). During the 165 million years of their existence, the pterosaurs were important piscivores (fish eaters) and, possibly, insectivores. Some achieved great size and unusual specialisations, especially in the Cretaceous.

The first pterosaurs from the Late Triassic, such as *Eudimorphodon* from northern Italy, have only come to light in the last 20 or so years of research. These early forms show all the particular characters of the group to which they belong: the wing membranes made from skin supported on a greatly elongated fourth finger, the short robust humerus (upper limb bone) and fused ulna and radius (forearm bones) which supported the flight muscles, the short body, the reduced and fused hip bones, five long toes (including a divergent toe 5, the outer toe), a long neck, and a large head with pointed jaws.

Animals like *Eudimorphodon* represent a common palaeontological enigma. It is the oldest known pterosaur, and it is well enough preserved, but it does

not tell us a great deal about the origin of the group: in most respects, it is a fully fledged pterosaur, and in no way a missing link between the ancestral small biped, a thecodontian, and the fully fledged Jurassic pterosaurs.

The key to the success of the pterosaurs is, of course, their wings. In all cases, the arm bones are relatively short and held close to the body, while the bulk of the leading edge (front supporting margin) of the wing is made of the enormously extended fourth finger. This finger contains the usual component bones, a metacarpal and four phalanges, seen in all typical reptiles, but each component is greatly stretched. (We have a metacarpal and three phalanges in our fourth finger.) The wing membrane ran along the entire length of the arm, to the tip of the fourth finger, and back in a curve toward the side of the body, possibly to the thigh region.

In the wrist, there is an additional small pointed bone at the front, the pteroid, which probably supported a second small wing membrane that ran from the wrist to the side of the neck. The pteroid may have operated to

One of the oldest known pterosaurs, Eudimorphodon *from the Late Triassic of northern Italy. The teeth are unusual, since there are several types: simple pointed ones at the front of the jaws, and three-pointed ones farther back.*

alter the shape of that membrane.

Eudimorphodon has a long narrow skull, with sharp teeth in the jaws. The eye orbits and other openings are large, thus making the skull rather lightweight – all of which are characteristics commonly seen in small carnivorous dinosaurs. The teeth are rather unusual, however, consisting of two main types: simple spikes at the front, and three-pronged spikes further back. *Eudimorphodon* was doubtless a fish-eater.

It is possible *Eudimorphodon* may have seized fish with the spike-like front teeth and held them firm with the back teeth while it swung them around into a position where they could be swallowed whole in one swift movement.

The pelvis (hip bones) of *Eudimorphodon*, as in other pterosaurs, is a solid little structure with strong, short bony elements that anchored various limb muscles. It seems that the legs worked like those of a small bipedal dinosaur, so that *Eudimorphodon* may have been able to run about quite efficiently on the ground, with its wings folded.

EARLY JURASSIC PTEROSAURS

The pterosaurs of the Triassic and Jurassic are generally referred to as rhamphorhynchoids, in order to distinguish them from the Cretaceous pterodactyloids. The rhamphorhynchoid group contains a diversity of forms and are a paraphyletic group, while the pterodactyloids have a single common ancestor shared with no other group, and so form a clade (page 111).

Until the mid-1970s, the oldest known pterosaur was *Dimorphodon* from the earliest Jurassic of southern England. The first specimen was found by the famous professional collector, Mary Anning, in 1828 (page 10), and one or two more have been found since in the coastal beds of the English Lias rocks that are probably considerably better known for their marine reptiles, the ichthyosaurs and plesiosaurs (pages 113, 124).

Dimorphodon has a vast head – it is typical of pterosaurs that the head is rather larger than the body. The massive high-sided jaws are lined with spaced-out pointed teeth that may have been used for eating insects, small land animals, or squid. The teeth at the front of the mouth are large, and those farther back are smaller and closer together, a pattern of differentiation similar to *Eudimorphodon*, but not so marked.

Dimorphodon has a long powerful neck (necessary to support the heavy head), a short trunk, and an extremely long tail. The tail is surrounded by numerous long rods of bone that would have acted to stiffen it, and it has been suggested that the tail was used as a kind of steering rod during flight, rather like the tail of a weathervane. The tail may also have been used as a balancing rod to assist in walking and running.

There has been considerable debate about the walking abilities of pterosaurs. Until recently, it was generally assumed that the best form of terrestrial locomotion they could manage was a sort of drunken tumbling. The legs were believed to have stuck out from the sides of the body at an odd angle, and the whole body was thought to be so unwieldy that all four limbs had to be used in walking: the feet and wrists touched the ground, and the long wing-finger pointed upward. In general, pterosaurs were pictured hanging upside down, like bats, from trees or cliff edges.

Debate continues about the precise fit of the legs into the hip bones: they may have pointed more upward and sideways than in the dinosaurs. However, it would seem rather odd if these animals were really so poor at walking, when one considers their probable close relationship to the dinosaurs, and the fact that they retained rel-

Pterosaurs show a number of major modifications of the skeleton, largely for flight. The shoulder and pelvic girdles are heavily fused to the adjacent vertebrae in advanced forms such as Pteranodon, to form the notarium and synsacrum respectively. The wing is supported largely by a greatly elongated fourth finger of each hand. The other fingers are much shorter, but could have been used in grasping. A new bony element, the pteroid, acted to control the shape of the small wing membrane in front of the arm. Many of the bones were hollow and had air holes.

THE ANATOMY OF A PTEROSAUR

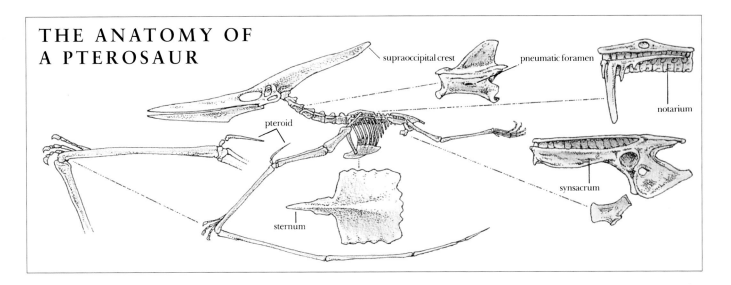

atively long legs. *Dimorphodon* has been pictured running at speed, with its massive head counterbalanced by the long tail behind. This seems a plausible model. It is rather more difficult to imagine one of the massive Late Cretaceous pterosaurs (which had wingspans of up to 50 feet or 15 metres, and huge heads but tiny tails) skipping along quite so boisterously!

PTEROSAURS OF THE LATE JURASSIC

Relatively little is known of pterosaurs from the Middle Jurassic, but some spectacularly diverse finds have come from the Late Jurassic. The Solnhofen Limestone of southern Bavaria in Germany has proved to be the best source of fine pterosaur skeletons over the years since the first example was found in 1784, by Cosmo Alessandro Collini (page 7). Four genera of pterosaurs have been reported from the Solnhofen Limestone: *Anurognathus*, *Germanodactylus*, *Pterodactylus*, and *Rhamphorhynchus*.

Anurognathus looked superficially like *Dimorphodon*, with a high-sided short skull and widely spaced teeth in its jaws. As in *Dimorphodon*, they may have been an adaptation to eating insects.

Rhamphorhynchus, another rhamphorhynchoid pterosaur, is rather better known. The head has long pointed jaws as in *Eudimorphodon*, but the teeth are rather different, showing more advanced features than are seen in many Cretaceous forms. The teeth are all similar, being shaped like sharp spikes, and they are well spaced; the front tips of the jaws are toothless. It is likely that *Rhamphorhynchus* was a fish-eater, and that it caught its prey by trawling the tip of its beak through the surface of the water, then seizing fish with the teeth farther back. It would then flap away to some height above the water surface, or even to land, to swallow the prey – just as sea birds do today. In swallowing, the fish in the mouth had to be freed from the teeth, rotated to a head-first position, and swallowed straight down. Considerable control, and sharp teeth, were necessary

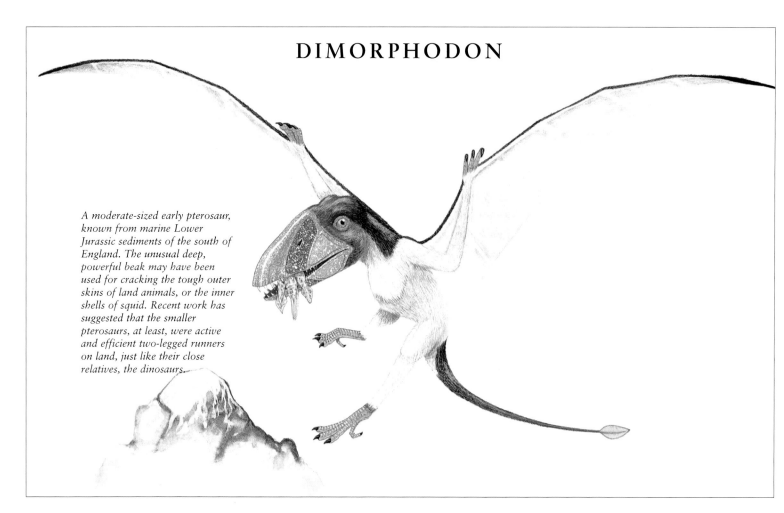

DIMORPHODON

A moderate-sized early pterosaur, known from marine Lower Jurassic sediments of the south of England. The unusual deep, powerful beak may have been used for cracking the tough outer skins of land animals, or the inner shells of squid. Recent work has suggested that the smaller pterosaurs, at least, were active and efficient two-legged runners on land, just like their close relatives, the dinosaurs.

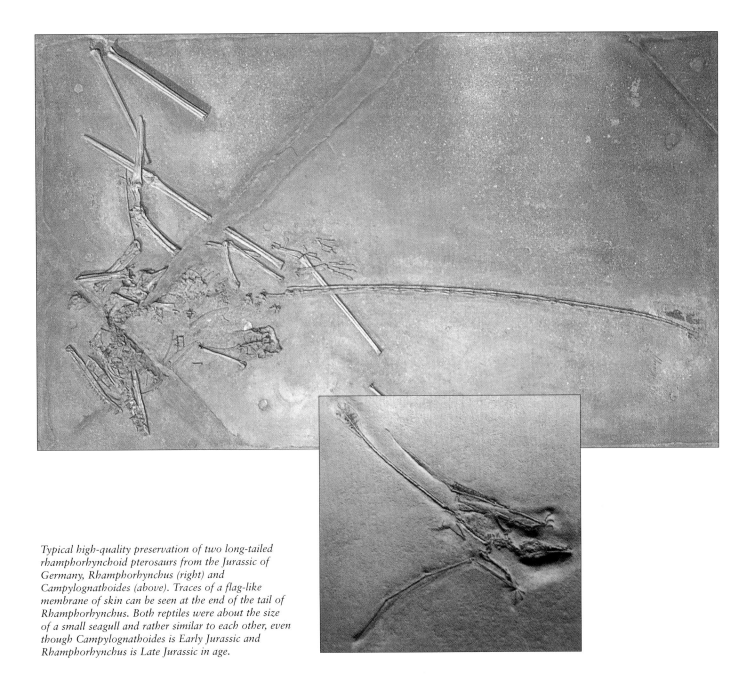

Typical high-quality preservation of two long-tailed rhamphorhynchoid pterosaurs from the Jurassic of Germany, Rhamphorhynchus (right) and Campylognathoides (above). Traces of a flag-like membrane of skin can be seen at the end of the tail of Rhamphorhynchus. Both reptiles were about the size of a small seagull and rather similar to each other, even though Campylognathoides is Early Jurassic and Rhamphorhynchus is Late Jurassic in age.

in order to prevent the struggling fishes from escaping.

Rhamphorhynchus has all the typical pterosaur features of the skeleton seen in earlier forms, but it is especially important because of the exquisite preservation of most of the fossils. Skeletons are generally complete, with all the bones connected and, most strikingly, the skin can often be seen as well. The shape of the wing membrane is quite clear in these specimens: it ran from the tip of the forelimb to attach along the side of the body, forming a much narrower wing, rather like a seagull, than many had assumed before. Additional skin membranes joined the front of the arm to the neck, and

there may have been narrow bands of loose skin behind the legs – but not, seemingly, the extensive webs often reconstructed between the legs and the tail. In addition, the skin outlines show the presence of a throat pouch in front of the neck, possibly a fish store for later swallowing or for the young. There is also a flag-like, diamond-shaped piece of skin at the end of the long tail, probably an additional "weathervane" for steering in flight.

Pterodactylus, found in the same deposits, shows some major advances that herald the evolution of the main pterodactyloid group, which dominated in the

continued on page 94

FLYING REPTILES OF THE LATE JURASSIC

One of the richest sources of fossil information about early flying reptiles, and the oldest birds, is the Solnhofen Limestone of southern Bavaria, dated as Portlandian (latest Jurassic, 150 million years ago). The deposits are those of a shallow marine lagoon, and the skeletons of pterosaurs, birds, and many other animals are exquisitely preserved.

The pterosaurs include the rhamphorhynchoid *Rhamphorhynchus* (left), with a long tail, and the pterodactyloids *Pterodactylus* (top right) and *Anurognathus* (bottom right), both with short tails. A famous animal from this locality is the earliest bird, *Archaeopteryx* (middle left).

How the world looked in this period

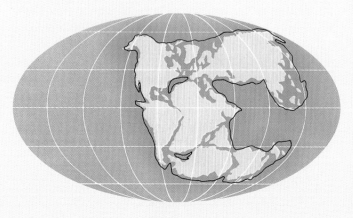

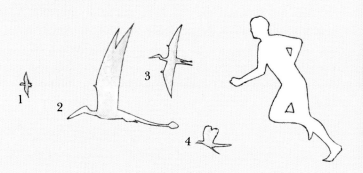

The Late Jurassic fliers were not as large as their Cretaceous relatives. Many pterosaurs, like Anurognathus (1), were tiny, Rhamphorhynchus (2) and Pterodactylus (3) were within the size spectrum of seagulls. Archaeopteryx (4) was on the scale of a pigeon.

Cretaceous. In overall shape, size, and habits, *Pterodactylus* was probably rather like *Rhamphorhynchus*: both were little larger than a pigeon, and they no doubt lived rather like small seagulls. However, *Pterodactylus* differs in having a larger skull with fewer teeth, a longer neck, and a much shorter tail. The fifth toe, a long diverging digit in rhamphorhynchoids, has almost disappeared, and the shoulder and hip girdles are more firmly fused to the backbone than in rhamphorhynchoids.

There were several species of *Pterodactylus* in the Solnhofen beds, the most unusual of which had long crests running down the mid-line of the skull. The crested pterodactyloids are often called *Germanodactylus*, and they seem to be close to the ancestry of all Cretaceous pterosaurs.

Why are pterosaurs so abundantly preserved, and so well preserved, in the Solnhofen beds? The rock in which the fossils are found is a very fine muddy limestone, yellowish-white in color, and deposited in almost perfectly horizontal layers with no irregularities. Indeed, so good is its quality that it was used for engraving delicate printing plates in the nineteenth century, hence its alternative name of lithographic limestone, and hence also the fact that exquisite fossils were found in the beds so early in the history of vertebrate palaeontology.

The Solnhofen Limestones were deposited in shallow seas, just offshore from a land mass covering most of

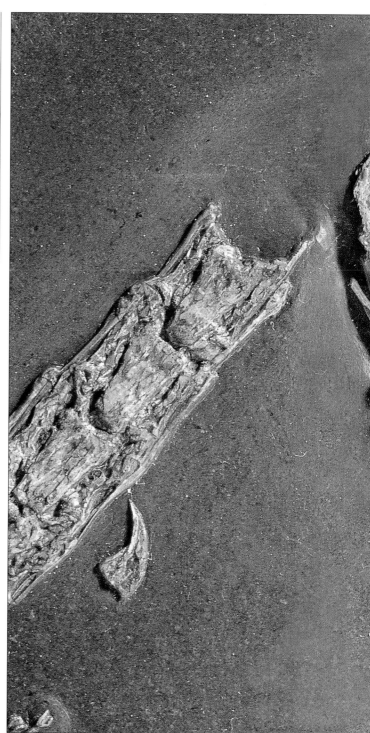

The skull of Dorygnathus *(right), a rhamphorhynchoid pterosaur from the Early Jurassic of Holzmaden, near Stuttgart, south-western Germany. The Holzmaden quarry is famous for its exquisite fossils of ichthyosaurs and crocodilians, as well as rarer plesiosaurs and pterosaurs. In all cases, the delicate bones are preserved complete and generally undisturbed; there are often traces of skin and other soft parts. The beautifully detailed preservation occurred because the fine black muds of Holzmaden were deposited very slowly in deep, oxygen-poor waters, so there were no scavengers.*

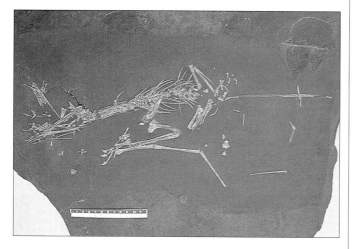

Skeleton of Dorygnathus *in which the skull and other bones have been slightly scattered by weak water currents. The vertebrae of the neck are broad and powerful, necessary to support the outsized head. The two long, narrow wing fingers run backwards on each side of the trunk.*

northern Europe. There were probably shallow lagoons that were not stirred by major currents or tides, and calcareous mud built up slowly over thousands of years. The fine sediment entombed jellyfish, worms, shellfish, bony fishes, sharks, and other marine animals, as well as turtles and crocodilians that occasionally took to the sea. Pieces of wood were washed in now and again, as were one or two skeletons of lizards and small dinosaurs. Flying animals such as pterosaurs – and of course the most famous fossil of all, the oldest known bird, *Archaeopteryx* – also fell in and became trapped and perfectly preserved.

CRETACEOUS PTERODACTYLOIDS

During the Cretaceous, pterosaurs became ever larger and more bizarre. The skull of *Pterodactylus* was about four inches (10 centimeters) long, while that of Ornithocheirus, a typical Early Cretaceous form, was 10 inches (25 centimeters), and that of *Pteranodon* from the Late Cretaceous reached six feet (1.8 meters).

Pterodaustro from the Early Cretaceous of Argentina is arguably the oddest-looking pterosaur. It has 400–500 long flexible teeth in each jaw which were used to catch microscopic plankton. The 'teeth' were probably made from a tough protein-based material, more like the baleen or whalebone of modern filter-feeding whales. *Pterodaustro* presumably flew low over the surface of the sea, pushing its massive head into the water. The teeth acted as a fine filter mesh in trapping thousands of small organisms, which could be licked off and swallowed. Certain modern birds filter small marine organisms in a similar way.

The best-known large pterosaur is probably *Pteranodon* found in the Late Cretaceous limestone deposits of the mid-western United States. The first fossil of *Pteranodon* was found in 1872, a rather uninspiring bone only eight inches (20 centimeters) long. It was sent to Othniel Charles Marsh (1831–99), who recognised it as the end of a finger bone of a pterosaur, but many times the size of forms such as *Pterodactylus* known at that time. Marsh is better known for his massive collections of dinosaurs and mammals, but he was willing to study any unusual vertebrate fossils that came his way. From this small piece of finger bone, Marsh speculated that its possessor would have had a wingspan of 20 feet (six meters) or more.

Over the next few years, Marsh's collectors gathered some 600 bones of *Pteranodon*, and it was possible to

PTERODAUSTRO

One of the oddest pterosaurs, a moderately large animal from the Early Cretaceous of Argentina. The long, curved, narrow jaws are lined with hundreds of thread-like "teeth" which appear to have been made of the tough protein keratin, rather than the dentine and enamel of normal teeth. Pterodaustro presumably trawled for plankton by skimming over the water and running its jaws just below the surface. It would lick off any small organisms trapped in the fine mesh.

Pterosaurs came in a great variety of shapes and sizes, although there was a trend toward increasing size during the Cretaceous. Triassic and Jurassic pterosaurs were no larger than today's seagulls. Those of the Early Cretaceous (Dsungaripterus) *reached albatross size, with wingspans of seven to nine feet (two or three meters). Those of the Late Cretaceous* (Pteranodon, Quetzalcoatlus) *were far larger than any known bird.*

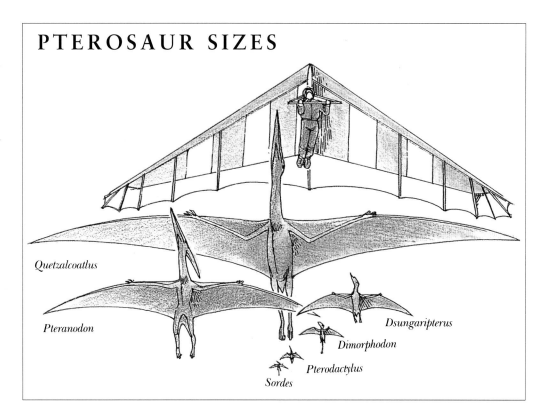

PTEROSAUR SIZES

Quetzalcoatlus

Pteranodon

Dsungaripterus

Dimorphodon

Pterodactylus

Sordes

present detailed reconstructions by the turn of the century. These confirmed a wingspan of up to almost 30 feet (eight meters) in different specimens.

Pteranodon's skull is longer than the torso, and its length is doubled by the long pointed crest at the back, formed by the supraoccipital bone. This unusual crest probably functioned like a weathervane to keep the head facing forward during flight. The jaws are toothless, but were probably covered with a sharp scaly beak in life, that would have been just as good as any teeth at cutting up fish. Not surprisingly, the cervical (neck) vertebrae are massive in order to support the vast head. Each of these vertebrae seems to have been hollow, an adaptation to reduce weight seen also in birds, and there was a pneumatic foramen (space) in the side of each, so that they probably contained air sacs.

The shoulder and hip girdles are remarkably reinforced and firmly stabilised. Each is fused to structures formed by the combination of vertebrae in the back and additional rods of bone alongside. The shoulder bones are attached to the girder-like notarium, which is composed of dorsal (back) vertebrate numbers 1–8, while the hip girdle is fused to the synsacrum, a complex structure containing ten dorsal and sacral (hip) vertebrae. In addition, the shoulder girdle is braced underneath the rib cage by firm attachments to the large sternum (breast bone). This massive strengthening and stabilization of the shoulders and hips must be related to the stresses of flight (shoulder girdle) and landing (hip girdle). Both of these movements must have created great forces in the skeleton, that might have dislocated the limb girdles if they had not been reinforced.

The limbs are essentially the same as those of the first pterosaurs, except for a few details. Whereas *Eudimorphodon* had six small bones in its wrist, *Pteranodon* has only two, and the ankle is similarly reduced. In addition, all the limb bones that bore the flying and walking muscles are relatively robust compared to the smaller Triassic and Jurassic pterosaurs, simply to cope with the problems of moving such a large animal.

FLYING GIANTS

Pteranodon was the largest known pterosaur until 1975, when James Lawson, a graduate student working in Texas, discovered the remains of an animal that may have been twice as large. His most important find was a single enormous humerus (upper arm bone) from a pterosaur which, when scaled against the known wing of *Pteranodon*, yielded an estimated span of up to 75 feet (22.5 metres)! The higher values are now generally discounted, and a range of wingspan of around 36–50 feet (11–15 metres) seems more likely. Since 1975, further isolated bones of this giant, since named *Quetzalcoatlus*, have come to light in Texas, as well as in the former USSR., Canada, Senegal in Africa, and Jordan. The Texas remains now include parts of the long, toothless jaws, and enough of the skull to suggest that the animal did not have a supraoccipital crest along the top of its skull. The neck is remarkably long, and each of the cervical (neck) vertebrae is a low tubular shape and some 12–16 inches (30–40 centimetres) in length. The rest of the skeleton appears to be a scaled-up *Pteranodon*.

Quetzalcoatlus is without doubt the largest flying animal ever to live on the Earth. It is three times as large as the largest known extinct flying birds (relatives of modern albatrosses and New World vultures), and it must have had more in common, aerodynamically, with a small aircraft than with any living flying animal. Working scale models of *Quetzalcoatlus* have shown that it could indeed fly. The wings were the right size to support the body, although they must have been close to the viable size limit for true flapping flight. *Quetzalcoatlus* had a body about the same size as that of a human, although it probably weighed about one-quarter as much because of weight-saving devices.

However, the wings had to be so long – simply to lift such a body from the ground and keep it aloft – that they faced problems of excessive stresses around the shoulder joint when they were flapped. Icarus, the hero of Greek legend who tried to fly with wings of feathers stuck into wax, would have needed an even greater wingspan than *Quetzalcoatlus* to achieve active flight!

PTEROSAUR FLIGHT

How did pterosaurs fly, and how good were they at it? Ever since the discovery of the first pterosaur specimens, there has been heated debate about their means of locomotion. After early discussion about whether they used their forelimbs in flight or in swimming, most palaeontologists accepted that they were flyers. The debate then shifted to the question of how well they could fly. Theories ranged from the idea that they were warm-blooded animals that flew just as well as modern bats and birds, to the notion that they were inefficient gliders that flung themselves from cliff-tops and hoped for the best. The Hollywood 'movie-star' pterosaur tends to

Most pterosaurs had low skulls with long, narrow snouts, and bulbous brain cases, to accommodate the visual and balance areas of the brains. Variations include high snouts, flexible teeth, or no teeth at all. The skulls are drawn to scale.

PTEROSAUR SKULLS

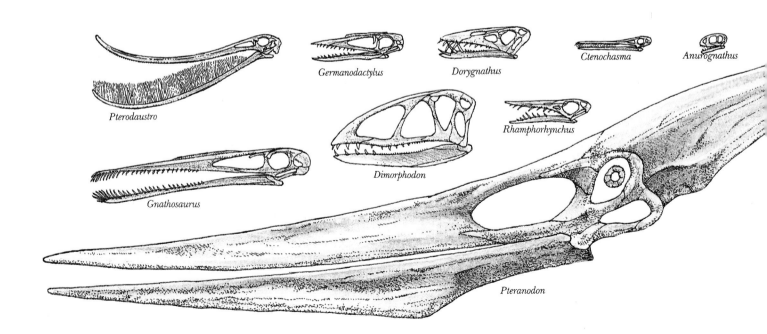

Pterodaustro

Germanodactylus

Dorygnathus

Ctenochasma

Anurognathus

Gnathosaurus

Dimorphodon

Rhamphorhynchus

Pteranodon

accept the latter interpretation, and is also dogged with flimsy wings that tear at the slightest gust of wind and an inability to walk on the ground other than by staggering and stumbling.

The evidence to solve such questions was accumulating even in the early part of the nineteenth century. Baron Georges Cuvier, the pre-eminent palaeontologist of the time, demonstrated that the long fourth finger supported a wing, and traces of such wings were seen in specimens from Solnhofen. In 1837, Hermann von Meyer (1810–69) reported that certain pterosaur bones were hollow and filled with air in life, a feature known otherwise only in birds. In the 1830s, hair was observed on the skin of some specimens, and certain naturalists speculated in the 1840s that the pterosaurs, like bats, had a high metabolic (body chemistry) rate, a further requisite for active flight.

This was confirmed in spectacular fashion by further discoveries this century, which have shown the presence of hair in a variety of Jurassic and Cretaceous pterosaurs. *Rhamphorhynchus*, for example, has over 10,000 hairs per square inch (about 20 per square millimetre), and each hair is one-eighth of an inch (two to three millimetres) long. The most remarkable fossils are those of *Sordes pilosus* ('hairy devil'), found in the Late Jurassic of Kazakhstan, Soviet Central Asia, in 1971. The hair covered the body and the upper part of the legs in a thick insulating pelt, and more sparsely over the wings and neck region.

The key evidence for active and efficient flight in pterosaurs is the presence of wings. If pterosaurs could not fly well, why did they have such splendid wings? Allied skeletal adaptations to flight include the hollow bones, the reinforced hip 'landing gear', and the streamlined head. The second key line of evidence for active flight is the possession of endothermy (internal temperature control), known otherwise only in birds, bats, and large insects.

The wing of a pterosaur is composed of skin that is attached to the side of the body and to the entire length of the arm and elongated flight finger. Older reconstructions show this flight membrane as a broad structure that joined to the neck at the front and well down the legs at the rear, as well as to the body. Additional large membranes were also reconstructed between the legs and tail. The Victorian recostruction of a pterosaur

QUETZALCOATLUS

The largest flying animal of all time, this highly successful giant pterosaur is known from North America, Africa, the Middle East, and the U.S.S.R. So far, complete skeletons have not been found, but enough is now known about it to produce a restoration. Quetzalcoatlus was the size of a small airplane, but it could have flapped its wings gently. Some palaeontologists have visualised these pterosaurs as giant vultures that circled high in the sky and descended to gorge on the carcasses of dinosaurs. It is more likely that they skimmed low over the sea and fed on fish snatched from just under the surface.

legs and tail. The Victorian recostruction of a pterosaur was thus rather like a kite or a parachute. But well-preserved specimens of *Rhamphorhynchus* and *Pterodactylus* have now shown that the pterosaur wing was a slender structure, rather like that of a gull (page 103). The wing membrane was reinforced by parallel stiff fibers or tight folds that indicate internal elastic fibres.

THE EVIDENCE FOR ACTIVE FLAPPING FLIGHT

A number of lines of evidence show that pterosaurs were powered or flapping flyers, and not simply gliders. Four key points concern comparison with living aerial vertebrates.

First, the flight membrane is well supported internally, within its thickness, and controlled by the forelimb. In living gliders, such as 'flying' fishes, lizards, squirrels, and so on, the flight membrane is an outgrowth of the body wall which lacks fine control in flight.

Second, the skeleton of the shoulder region is highly modified for powerful up-and-down flapping movements, and there are large flanges and projections on the bones for attachment of the flight muscles.

Third, the front limb itself is highly modified for active flight, both in terms of the flight membrane and the muscle attachments.

Fourth, the wing stroke in pterosaur flight was similar to that of birds and bats. In modern gliding vertebrates, the shoulder and front limb can move in many directions, but in pterosaurs, birds, and bats, the range of movements is restricted to those used in flight.

It has been possible to reconstruct the flight muscles of pterosaurs, and they turn out to be very similar in action to those of birds. The main power stroke, the downstroke, was produced by the pectoralis muscle, which was anchored at one end in a broad area over the sternum (breast bone), and at the other end on the underside of the humerus (upper arm bone). Contraction of the pectoralis pulled the wing down. The upstroke was powered by a smaller and rather more complex muscle, the supracoracoideus. It was also attached to the sternum, but at its other end it joined the top surface of the humerus, having passed over a complex "pulley" system at the shoulder joint. Contraction of the supracoracoideus, although a downward pull, therefore lifted the wing up, because of this pulley sys-

tem. In some ways, the system is like the pivoted rods that lift the lid of a trash pedal can when you press down on the pedal.

Pterosaurs probably took off from trees or cliffs, or after a short run to pick up speed. Even in the giant members of the group, the take-off run was at low speed – about 13 feet (four metres) per second in *Pteranodon*. When landing, the stalling speed for pterosaurs was lower than for birds of the same weight. This meant that they could fly more slowly without suddenly tipping over and falling to the ground, and so they were more maneuverable at low speeds. Even so, landing was probably awkward for the larger pterosaurs, just as it is for large birds today. No wonder they needed reinforced hip girdles to withstand the impacts.

Pterosaurs were truly the flying giants of the Cretaceous. Another group of flying vertebrates evolved to occupy smaller-sized ecological niches from the Late Jurassic onward. These were the birds.

ARCHAEOPTERYX, A FLYING DINOSAUR

The first evidence that birds existed during the Mesozoic era was a single feather, found in the Solnhofen Limestones in 1860. It was described one year later by Hermann von Meyer, who named it *Archaeopteryx lithographica* ('ancient wing from the lithographic stone'). Meanwhile, a complete skeleton with feather impressions had also been found in the Solnhofen Limestones, and von Meyer published a description of this, too, one month later. This specimen rapidly became a cause célebre in Germany, and England too, where it proved a particularly timely discovery. Charles Darwin's On the Origin of Species had been published in 1859, and the public and scientists alike were agog with his revolutionary ideas.

Darwin confirmed the view already held by many palaeontologists: that evolution had occurred. In other words, living organisms had passed through a series of different forms over vast periods of time, and that these stages in the sequence of evolution could be traced in the fossil record. Darwin's chief contribution was to propose a mechanism, which he called natural selection, to explain the pattern of evolution. This is the idea that the variation seen between individuals of a species is a source of material, upon which the forces of natural selection act, depending upon environmental influences. Over time, natural selection has shaped the history of to find crucial evidence for evolution by natural selection in the fossil record. What was needed was clear palaeontological evidence that one major group of animals had turned into another – in other words, an intermediate form or missing link. Archaeopteryx could not have been found at a better time!

The complete fossilised skeleton was bought from the quarryman by a local doctor and amateur fossil collector, Carl Häberlein. He soon recognised its potential value and made its presence known to interested scientists. However, he would not let any of them make detailed notes or drawings, and hence all kinds of rumours circulated about just how important the "feathered dinosaur" fossil was. The local palaeontological museum in Munich might have bought the specimen, but the money was not forthcoming. Its curator, Andreas Wagner, was a Biblical creationist who would not accept evolution, nor of course the potential importance of the new German fossil. Häberlein then offered this entire collection of fossils, including the new skeleton, to the British Museum in London, and they eventually obtained it for £700. This was a great sum of money for the time, and it represented the entire purchasing budget of the museum for two years. However, bear in mind that in the 1820s, Mary Anning was able to sell her fossil ichthyosaurs and plesiosaurs for £150 or more. In comparison, the price paid for Archaeopteryx, and all H¨äberlein's other fossils, seems a bargain.

The London specimen, as it is now known, was studied and described by several leading paleontologists, and it soon came to feature strongly in debates about evolution. A second complete skeleton of Archaeopteryx was found in 1877, and it passed to Carl Häberlein's son, Ernst. He put it on the market, demanding a much higher price than his father had received for the London specimen. It became an object of German national pride that they should acquire the fossil, and in the end the Prussian State paid DM20,000 and lodged the specimen in the Humboldt Museum. It is now referred to as the Berlin specimen, and it shows all parts of the body, including the skull and some very fine distinctive feather impressions.

Four more Archaeopteryx skeletons have come to light since 1877. Three were discovered this century, in 1951, 1955, and 1987. The other was recognised as

continued on page 104

The arm and wing of Archaeopteryx (below) showing a structure that is intermediate between the arm of a theropod dinosaur and the wing of a modern bird. The bones are very dinosaurian in shape and layout: the single upper-arm bone (humerus); the pair of slender forearm bones (radius and ulna); and the three long fingers, each with a substantial claw. The close dinosaurian relatives of birds also had long, narrow hands with only three fingers. The flight feathers spread out below the arm; they are attached to the humerus, radius, and ulna

The first feather of Archaeopteryx to be found (left), the 1860 specimen, now in the Humboldt Museum, Berlin. Two inches (six centimeters) long, this feather is virtually indistinguishable from the feather of a modern flying bird. The long quill-like vane is clearly preserved, and the distribution of barbs on each side is asymmetrical – clear evidence that it is the feather of a flyer (flightless birds have symmetrical feathers).

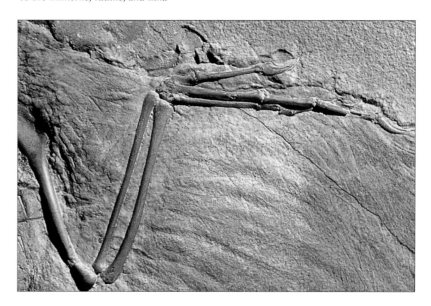

PTEROSAUR FLIGHT

Since the first discovery of pterosaurs in the mid-eighteenth century, palaeontologists and biologists have debated their flying abilities. At first, some thought that the wings were actually paddles, used in a way analogous to the wing-paddles of penguins. However, it was clear, after the work of Georges Cuvier in the early nineteenth century, that the wings were for flying.

Since then, there has been debate about just how well the pterosaurs could have flown. Were they inferior, creaking flyers that just about managed to stay aloft, to be outshone by any bird? This is the popular Hollywood conception! Recent analyses of pterosaurian anatomy, including studies of their soft parts, along with biomechanical calculations, have suggested that they were highly efficient flyers – and this includes even the Late Cretaceous monsters!

A nineteenth-century view of the appearance of Rhamphorhynchus *(above), in which the wing membrane was a substantial structure that extended well back along the legs, and between them. This gave a large surface area of wing for flight, but made walking awkward. Modern views of the wing shape are very different.*

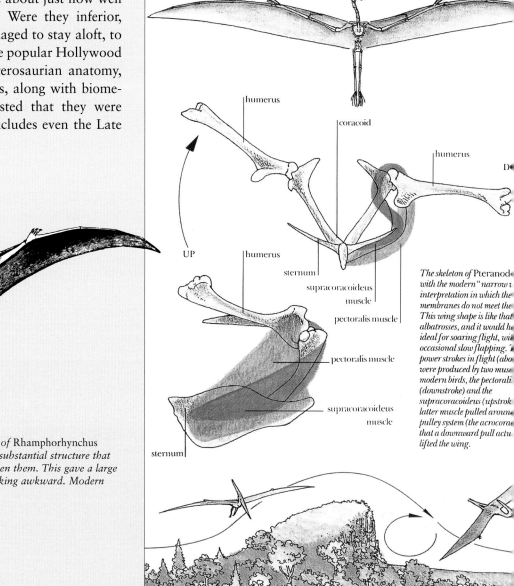

humerus

coracoid

humerus

D

humerus

UP

sternum

supracoracoideus muscle

pectoralis muscle

pectoralis muscle

supracoracoideus muscle

sternum

The skeleton of Pteranod with the modern "narrow interpretation in which the membranes do not meet the This wing shape is like that albatrosses, and it would he ideal for soaring flight, wi occasional slow flapping. power strokes in flight (abo were produced by two muse modern birds, the pectorali (downstroke) and the supracoracoideus (upstrok latter muscle pulled aroun pulley system (the acrocora that a downward pull actu lifted the wing.

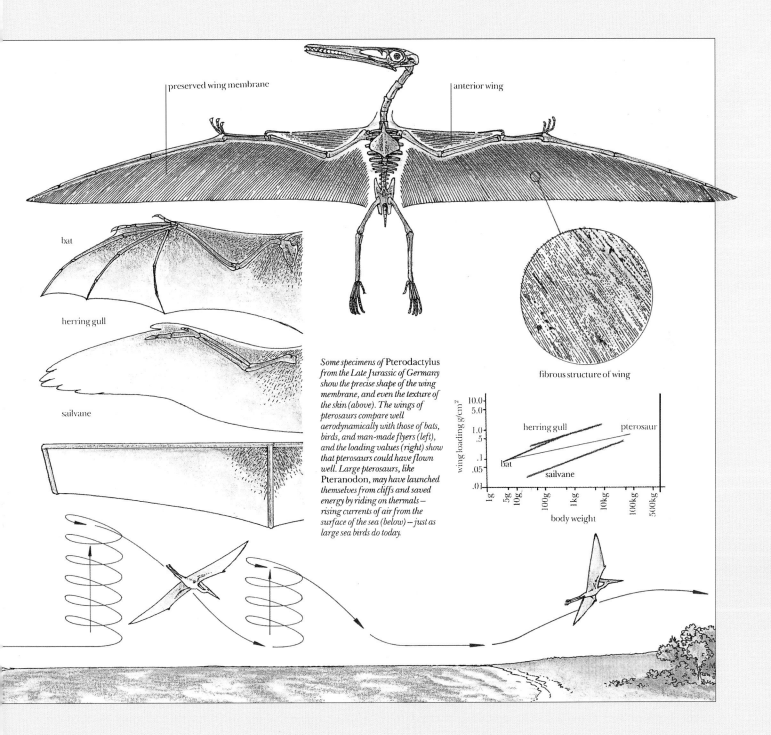

preserved wing membrane

anterior wing

bat

herring gull

sailvane

fibrous structure of wing

Some specimens of Pterodactylus *from the Late Jurassic of Germany show the precise shape of the wing membrane, and even the texture of the skin (above). The wings of pterosaurs compare well aerodynamically with those of bats, birds, and man-made flyers (left), and the loading values (right) show that pterosaurs could have flown well. Large pterosaurs, like* Pteranodon, *may have launched themselves from cliffs and saved energy by riding on thermals — rising currents of air from the surface of the sea (below) — just as large sea birds do today.*

herring gull
pterosaur
bat
sailvane
body weight
wing loading g/cm²

10.0
5.0
1.0
.5
.1
.05
.01

1g 5g 10g 100g 1kg 10kg 100kg 500kg

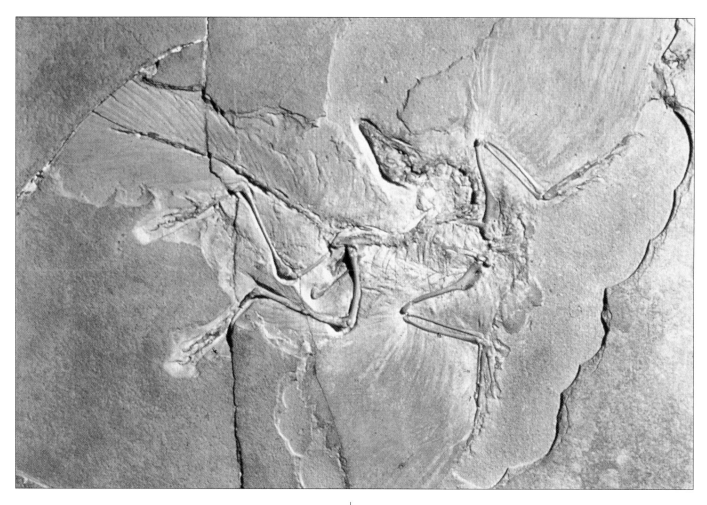

The most valuable fossil in the world? The Berlin specimen of Archaeopteryx, *found in 1877, and purchased for DM 20,000. This is the most complete of the six fossil skeletons of the world's first known bird.*

Archaeopteryx in 1970, but collected much earlier – in 1855. This last specimen consists only of partial remains, with very poor feather impressions, and was first identified as a pterosaur. It languished in the museum in Haarlem, Holland, labelled as such, and hence not very highly regarded, until its true nature was discerned by a visiting American paleontologist.

The skeletons of *Archaeopteryx* are exquisitely preserved in the fine-grained limestones formed from the bottom sediments of the ancient Solnhofen lagoon. They are accompanied by a diverse fauna of marine and terrestrial animals, as well as pterosaurs (page 97). It would seem that *Archaeopteryx* lived in an area of open plains with sparse vegetation, interspersed with busy conifers, and other primitive plants. No doubt, it flew out over the lagoon in pursuit of insects, and occasional individuals became waterlogged or trapped and fell to the bottom and drowned. The carcasses floated to

the surface, buoyed up by the gases of decomposition, and drifted with the belly area uppermost, and the head, wings, and limbs dangling. Eventually, the guts burst and the carcasses sank to the bottom, where they rested on their sides, wings and legs sprawling, head bent back by contraction of the neck muscles and ligaments, and the long feathers of the wings and tail arrayed on all sides. These feathers were firmly attached to the bones, as they are in modern birds, and hence did not drift away from the carcass. Further mud was deposited, slowly covering the skeleton.

COULD *ARCHAEOPTERYX* BE A HOAX?

The remarkable quality of preservation of the *Archaeopteryx* specimens has led to doubts concerning their authenticity. The most recent suggestions of this kind were made in 1987 by Sir Fred Hoyle, the noted British cosmologist and physicist. He argued that *Archaeopteryx* was a composite of the genuine fossils of a small bipedal dinosaur with the addition of artificial feather imprints made by Carl and Ernst Häberlein, to enhance the value of their fossils. These gentlemen were supposed to have spread a fine cement of limestone grains and water around the bones, pressed in modern bird feathers, and then allowed the whole thing to harden.

Of course, the proponents of such an opinion had been misled by the view that many non-palaeontologists hold, that fossils are always rather poorly preserved. This is not the case. Since 1987, Hoyle and other advocates of the forgery theory have been unable to show how anyone could produce such high-fidelity imprints of feathers without leaving evidence of the counterfeit. In addition, they have been unable to say how the Haberleins could have forged the skeletons of *Archaeopteryx* found after their death – and one even after the publication of the accusations. Finally, of course, they were either unaware of the spectacular array of exquisitely preserved fossils in the Solnhofen Limestones (soft-bodied worms and jellyfish, fish guts and skin, pterosaur hair, and so on), or they chose to ignore them – or are all these other fossils counterfeits, as well? In palaeontology, as in much of life, the truth is often more spectacular than any fiction!

THE ORIGIN OF THE BIRDS

What is *Archaeopteryx*? Is it a bird, or is it a reptile? If it is a bird, what did it evolve from? It turns out that most palaeontologists in the 1870s had the right idea, and much that has followed since is pure obfuscation.

Archaeopteryx is a bird since it has feathers. It is an arbitrary decision to draw the line that separates birds from reptiles at the first occurrence of feathers, but this represents everyone's understanding of what a bird is, and it is unlikely that a complex dermal (skin-derived) structure like a feather could have evolved more than once.

Archaeopteryx was recognised early on as a 'missing link', however, because it retains a number of primitive "reptilian" characters that are absent in modern birds: possession of teeth, separate fingers with claws in the hand, no ossified sternum, and a long, bony tail. But which group of reptiles is closest to the ancestry of the birds?

Victorian scientists sought the origin of the birds among the lizards, the pterosaurs, and the dinosaurs, with most influential opinion favoring the dinosaurs. In the early twentieth century, however, a compromise view gained ground: birds arose much earlier than the Late Jurassic, indeed they appeared in the Late Triassic, directly from the thecodontians. This view held sway until the 1970s, when a variety of hypotheses for the origin of birds was put forward.

One hypothesis was that they arose from a common ancestor with the crocodilians, because of detailed resemblances in the braincase region of the skull.

A second is that they arose from a thecodontian, probably something close to *Ornithosuchus* (page 81).

A third possibility is that they shared a direct common ancestor with mammals, because of their warm-bloodedness and other features.

Fourth, it has been suggested that they arose from a small, bipedal, flesh-eating type of dinosaur.

The last of these views has prevailed. *Archaeopteryx* and later birds share many detailed resemblances with the carnivorous (theropod) dinosaurs in the shape and structure of the skull, hands, hip girdle, and legs. Many of these similarities are so striking that it is hard to distinguish individual bones of Archaeopteryx from those of small, advanced theropods. Indeed, it has been rightly said that, without its feathers, it would be very hard to prove that *Archaeopteryx* was not itself a small theropod. But could it fly?.

FEATHERS AND THE ORIGIN OF FLIGHT

It is now believed that Archaeopteryx could fly nearly as efficiently as a modern bird. After all, as with the pterosaurs, if it could not, then why did it have wings, feathers, and warm-bloodedness?

Nevertheless, some experts have argued recently that *Archaeopteryx* could not have flown, since it lacks two bony structures that appear to be crucial for flight in modern birds: a bony sternum (breast bone) for attachment of the great flight muscles (pectoralis and supracoracoideus), and the specialised pulley system at the shoulder joint seen in modern birds and in pterosaurs (page 102). In addition, it was noted that the shoulder girdle and front limb of *Archaeopteryx* seem to be too weak to withstand the stresses of wing flapping.

Two strong lines of evidence seem to confirm that *Archaeopteryx* was indeed a strong, powered flyer. First, the absence of a bony sternum need not have been a problem. The pectoralis muscle could just as well have been connected to the wishbone area and ribs. Indeed, bats lack a substantial bony sternum and yet they manage to fly perfectly well. Second, the feathers have an asymmetrical shape in which the central quill portion is off-center, just as in modern flying birds – instead of the symmetrical shape seen in ostriches and other non-flyers.

The origins of flight in birds, as in pterosaurs, can only be speculative. There are two main current theories, in which flight arose either "from the ground up" or "from the trees down," although a diversity of other views has been held in the past.

BIRD EVOLUTION

Scattered bird fossils are known from the Early Cretaceous period in various parts of the world, but well preserved fossils occur only from the latter part of the Late Cretaceous onward. During the Cretaceous, all the primitive 'reptilian' features of *Archaeopteryx* were successively lost: the teeth, the clawed hand, the long bony tail. Modern bird characters appeared: the deep, bony sternum (the keel of the breast region in a baked chicken or turkey), the fused hip bones, the reduced, stump-like, bony tail, and the fused bones of the lower leg.

Modern bird groups appeared in Tertiary times, dur-

THE ORIGINS OF BIRDS

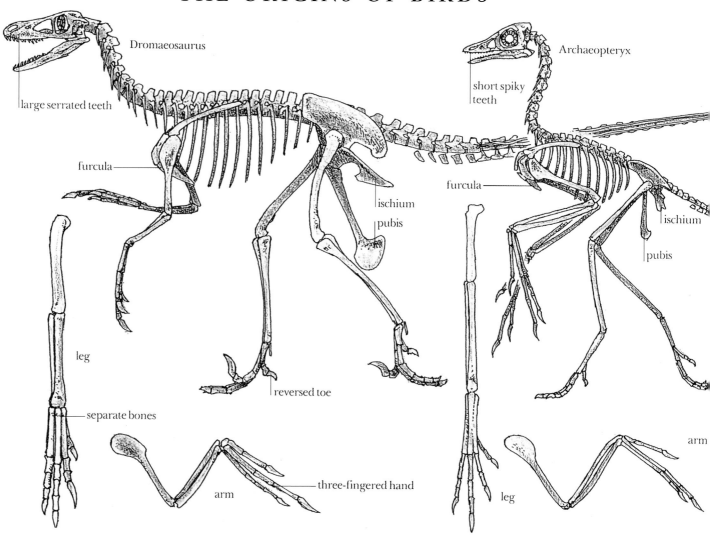

Dromaeosaurus

large serrated teeth

furcula

ischium

pubis

leg

separate bones

reversed toe

arm

three-fingered hand

Archaeopteryx

short spiky teeth

furcula

ischium

pubis

arm

leg

ing the last 65 million years after the extinction of the dinosaurs and pterosaurs, although some palaeontologists identify early flightless birds (ancestors of the ostriches and cassowaries) and early shore birds in the Late Cretaceous. Bird evolution has proved hard to analyse, because fossils are relatively rare and usually very incomplete.

If we regard birds and mammals as direct reptilian derivatives, then we must recognize the continuing success of reptile descendants as flyers, despite the loss of various gliding forms in the Permian and Triassic, and the loss of the pterosaurs at the end of the Cretaceous period.

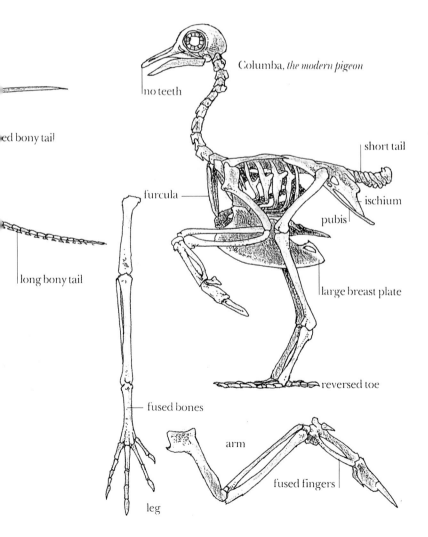

ed bony tail

Columba, *the modern pigeon*

no teeth

short tail

furcula

ischium

pubis

long bony tail

large breast plate

reversed toe

fused bones

arm

leg

fused fingers

In many respects, the skeleton of Archaeopteryx *is more similar to that of the medium-sized theropod dinosaur* Dromaeosaurus, *from the Early Cretaceous of North America, than the skeleton of a modern pigeon. The arms and legs have changed relatively little, although the modern bird has lost some fingers, and the bones are more fused. In order to become a modern bird,* Archaeopteryx *would have to lose its tail and fingers, grow a deep keel in the chest region and a longer neck, and fuse the pelvis into a sturdier, shock-absorbing structure.*

CHAPTER

5

REPTILES OF THE SEAS

The reptiles became adapted to life in the sea many times during their evolution. They moved back into the sea from the land in order to exploit the rich sources of food there – shellfish, fish, and plankton – and many became highly modified to an aquatic existence. It is remarkable how many reptile groups evolved marine forms quite independently of each other: mesosaurs in the Permian; ichthyosaurs, nothosaurs, placodonts, and others in the Triassic; ichthyosaurs, plesiosaurs, and crocodilians in the Jurassic; and these groups plus mosasaurs in the Cretaceous.

FISHES OF THE CARBONIFEROUS AND PERMIAN

The whole course of reptilian evolution during the Carboniferous and Permian periods had been toward increasing terrestrialisation: major physiological, anatomical, and behavioral changes allowed reptiles to break cleanly with the need to live and breed in water (Chapters 1, 2). The reason for their return to the water, as mentioned above, seems to have been simply the vast food sources in the seas, which were otherwise not exploited.

The fishes of the Devonian (pages 22–23) consisted of

various heavily armored agnathans and placoderms, as well as the first chondrichthyans (sharks and rays) and osteichthyans (bony fishes). Some of the lobe-finned bony fish and certain giant placoderms preyed on the smaller fish, and there was a relatively complete food chain. However, after the Devonian, some of the top predators – the large placoderms, in particular – had died out. Thus there were no animals large enough to exploit the burgeoning, newly evolving groups of unarmored chondrichthyans and osteichthyans.

The Carboniferous chondrichthyans included a vari-

REPTILES OF THE SEAS

Two images of the spectacular fossil reptiles of the seas. Plesiosaurs (long necks) and an ichthyosaur swim in the shallow waters of the Early Jurassic, in an 1885 reconstruction from a popular book (right). The two beautifully preserved specimens are of the nothosaur Serpianosaurus, *from the Middle Triassic marine sediments of Monte San Giorgio, Switzerland (opposite page). An adult specimen lies stretched from left to right, and the skeleton of a juvenile crosses it. The head of the latter lies at the bottom of the slab in the middle, and it is partly missing. Note the very long tails and the thickened ribs.*

ety of shark-like fishes, often armed with spines associated with the fins on their backs. Some, like *Cladoselache* from the Late Devonian and Early Carboniferous, were sleek animals like modern dogfishes, with large pectoral (front) fins and a long tail to produce the thrust for rapid swimming. Others, however, were much more unusual, as recent finds have shown from the black, shallow-marine mudstones of central Scotland and the American Midwest.

The most remarkable Carboniferous sharks were the stethacanthids. Although isolated remains have been known for over a century, their full anatomy has only become clear recently. *Stethacanthus*, three feet (one metre) long, is now known from nearly complete specimens from Scotland and Montana. It has a strange spine just behind its head which is shaped like a shaving brush!

The spine stands nearly vertical and is topped by dozens of small teeth. This unwieldy structure must have had an important function, although it was present in both males and females and was thus probably not associated with mating displays. It has been suggested that the spine and its teeth may have been used to scare off potential predators: when *Stethacanthus* lay partially buried in the mud, the two toothed areas – one in the mouth and one on the top of the head, borne on the spine – would have mimicked a vast, gaping mouth, as of some giant and deadly predator. This may have served to discourage any larger would-be carnivore seeking to eat this shark.

The bony fishes also evolved rapidly in the Carboniferous and Permian, and one early group became especially abundant. These were the paleonisciforms, like *Cheirolepis* from the Devonian period and *Cheirodus* from the Carboniferous. They were often small and appear to have lived in large schools, judging by the fact that their remains are often found in large numbers in single sedimentary rock layers. The paleonisciforms look superficially like modern bony fish such as herrings or salmon, but they belong to a more primitive stage of evolution. The main differences are that the paleonisciform body was covered with a regular array of thick, diamond-shaped bony scales; the lobes of the tail were not symmetrical in side view; and the jaws opened and shut like a simple hinge. Modern bony fish have wafer-thin scales, a symmetrical tail, and a complex jaw apparatus which makes the mouth pout forward some distance when it opens..

Despite the expanding diversity of succulent chondrichthyans and osteichthyans in Carboniferous and Permian oceans, it was some 100 million years after the reptiles' ancestors first stepped onto the land, before they ventured to dip their toes in the sea again. Even then, the first marine reptiles were a rather small-scale, tentative experiment.

THE MESOSAURS

Mesosaurus from the Early Permian of Brazil and southern Africa is the oldest known marine reptile. It is represented by abundant well-preserved skeletons that show a slender animal, three feet (one meter) in length, with a long neck and an enormously elongated, flat-sided tail which was clearly used for propulsion through the water. The limb girdles are reduced in size, which suggests that they did not support the weight of the

MESOSAURUS

The first known reptile to venture into the sea as a fish-eater, Mesosaurus *was a representative of a small, short-lived group from the Early Permian. Although it is faintly reminiscent of a fish-eating crocodilian,* Mesosaurus *belonged to a much more primitive group, of uncertain affinities. It was also much smaller than it seems, being only one foot (30 centimeters) long, and therefore only able to prey on the smallest fish.*

MARINE REPTILES

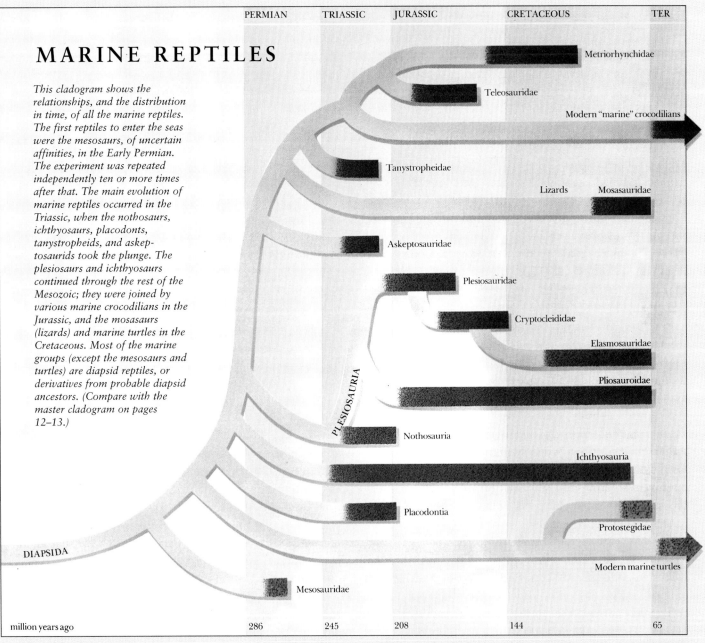

This cladogram shows the relationships, and the distribution in time, of all the marine reptiles. The first reptiles to enter the seas were the mesosaurs, of uncertain affinities, in the Early Permian. The experiment was repeated independently ten or more times after that. The main evolution of marine reptiles occurred in the Triassic, when the nothosaurs, ichthyosaurs, placodonts, tanystropheids, and askeptosaurids took the plunge. The plesiosaurs and ichthyosaurs continued through the rest of the Mesozoic; they were joined by various marine crocodilians in the Jurassic, and the mosasaurs (lizards) and marine turtles in the Cretaceous. Most of the marine groups (except the mesosaurs and turtles) are diapsid reptiles, or derivatives from probable diapsid ancestors. (Compare with the master cladogram on pages 12–13.)

PERMIAN TRIASSIC JURASSIC CRETACEOUS TER

Metriorhynchidae
Teleosauridae
Modern "marine" crocodilians
Tanystropheidae
Lizards Mosasauridae
Askeptosauridae
Plesiosauridae
Cryptocleididae
Elasmosauridae
Pliosauroidea
PLESIOSAURIA
Nothosauria
Ichthyosauria
Placodontia
Protostegidae
DIAPSIDA
Modern marine turtles
Mesosauridae

million years ago 286 245 208 144 65

body on land very often; the hands and feet are expanded as paddles. The skull is elongate and superficially crocodile-like, with the eye sockets set well back. The long, slim jaws are lined with remarkable pointed, needle-thin teeth that interlock with each other as the jaws close. This formed a kind of cage or straining device that allowed *Mesosaurus* to take a mouthful of planktonic organisms or small fish, and strain the water out before swallowing.

The mesosaurs were a short-lived, although locally successful, group. They became celebrated among geologists since they provided strong evidence for continental drift. Skeletons of identical species were found in similar rocks both on the western side of southern Africa and in eastern Brazil. When the continents of Africa and South America were pushed together into the positions they presumably occupied during the Permian (that is, with no Atlantic Ocean intervening), the sedimentary rocks must have joined to form one continuous layer, and the former true distribution of *Mesosaurus* is logically restored. If it is argued that continental drift has not occurred, and that the land masses occupied their present positions in the Permian, then it would be hard to explain how a small coastal animal like *Mesosaurus* could have travelled back and forth across the Atlantic.

In Triassic seas

Reptiles began to exploit the life of the sea with a vengeance in the Triassic period, starting some 245 million years ago. They continued to do so for the rest of the Mesozoic Era, until they, together with the dinosaurs, became extinct 65 million years ago.

Triassic coastal waters were inhabited by a variety of molluscs (shellfish such as bivalves and snail-like gastropods), worms, corals, sponges, and other invertebrates, not unlike those in today's warm seas. In addition, the first modern-style oysters and limpets came on the scene and provided a new food source on the rocky shores. Swimming above the seabed were coiled molluscs called ammonoids. The Triassic ammonoids were shaped rather like the modern pearly nautilus, and the animal inside the shell was no doubt a similarly succulent, tentacled, octopus-like creature.

There were also major new fish groups. The main shark types were the hybodonts, fast-swimming animals that appear to show advances over their Carboniferous and Permian relatives. *Hybodus*, a typical example, had a streamlined body with powerful muscles along the sides, that bent the body into sinuous waves to produce the propulsive thrust when swimming. It had large pectoral fins, like most modern sharks, which functioned mainly in steering and stabilisation. A variety of tooth types lined its jaws; some were high and pointed, while others were low, which suggests that *Hybodus* fed on a broad range of prey, ranging from other fishes to bottom-living crabs and shrimp.

The paleonisciforms continued to form a significant part of Triassic fish life, but new groups of bony fish, collectively termed the "holosteans," arose during this period. Particularly important in lakes and inland seas

during the later parts of the Triassic were the semionotids, such as *Semionotus*. This was a small, actively swimming fish, which had a symmetrical tail fin, and more complex jaws than those of the paleonisciforms.

Semionotids occur in great diversity in some areas. A spectacular array of forms has been found in the Newark Group lakes, that stretched along most of the eastern seaboard of North America during the Late Triassic and Early Jurassic. Thousands of specimens have been collected by careful bed-by-bed sampling, which show how the lakes were occupied by 10-20 species of semionotid at any one time. The species seem to have evolved rapidly as the lakes formed, evaporated, and dried out, then reformed again periodically. Whole fish faunas were wiped out by the catastrophic drying episodes; however, surviving semionotids moved in from elsewhere when the lakes refilled, and they soon radiated into a diverse range of species again.

The first fish lizards

The first reptiles that were completely adapted to life in the sea were the ichthyosaurs (fish lizards). They had a streamlined dolphin-like body with no neck, a long snout, limb paddles, and a fish-like tail. At one time, they were thought to arise in the Middle Triassic, but one or two rare forms from Spitzbergen and Japan have now been found in the Early Triassic.

Ichthyosaurs must have evolved from fully terrestrial reptiles, and the transition period must have been fairly long, since even the rare Early Triassic types are highly aquatic in adaptations. Yet no intermediate fossils have so far been found. So where did they come from? At one time, it was thought that the ichthyosaurs had their origin during the very earliest phase of reptile evolution,

Mesosaurus, *a tiny Permian marine reptile (below). Even in this salamander-sized animal, the ribs are greatly thickened, a characteristic of most marine reptiles.*

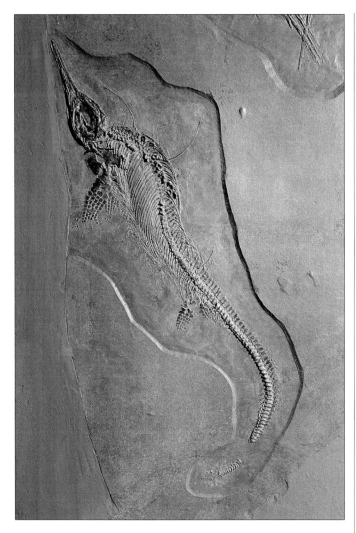

Mixosaurus, a successful Middle Triassic ichthyosaur, is known from most parts of the world (opposite page), This splendid specimen, from the marine beds of the Monte San Giorgio, Switzerland, shows the long, narrow snout and large eye, streamlined body, long tail with down-curved end, and paddles. Even in this early ichthyosaur, all traces of the group's land-living ancestors have disappeared. The fingers in the paddles have lost their definition, and Mixosaurus could not have moved at all on land.

separate fingers that must have been present in the terrestrial hands and feet of their ancestor. The neck is short, the back long. The skull is fully ichthyosaurian, with many peg-like teeth, large orbits (eye sockets), and a single temporal fenestra – the so-called euryapsid skull pattern seen also in nothosaurs, placodonts, and plesiosaurs (page 125). Later ichthyosaurs show advances over the skull shape of *Grippia* in that the snout becomes longer, the orbit larger, and the bones at the back of the skull more "crowded" toward the rear.

Middle Triassic ichthyosaurs such as *Mixosaurus* show these advances, as well as others. For example, the paddle has shorter limb bones and many more phalanges (individual finger bones) than in any land-living tetrapod. Some specimens of *Mixosaurus* are so well preserved in the fine-grained black mudstones laid down in central Europe's shallow seas that outlines of the body shape may be seen in the form of a thin carbonaceous film of preserved skin. This has shown, for example, that an ichthyosaur had a fin in the middle of the back, rather like the menacing dorsal fin of a shark, supported entirely by tough connective tissue. In the absence of bone within this dorsal fin, a normally preserved fossil shows no trace of it. The Middle Triassic ichthyosaur carcasses apparently fell to a sea floor that was rich in organic matter (hence the black color of the mudstones), but low in oxygen. Hence, scavenging organisms could not survive near the sea bottom, and the carcasses were little disturbed as they were covered by a gentle rain of sediment from above.

Some Late Triassic ichthyosaurs reached enormous size, attaining lengths as great as 50 feet (15 metres). Their huge skeletons show long bullet-shaped heads, teeth only at the front of the snout, vast rounded rib cages, and very long paddles. These ecological precursors of the great whales (which are, of course, mammals) may have fed on other marine reptiles, or on ammonoids – just as modern sperm whales feed on squid and nautiloids. The ichthyosaurs of the Late Triassic included a diversity of smaller forms which evolved further during the Jurassic and Cretaceous periods, but they rarely again achieved such giant proportions as they had in earlier times.

THE NOTHOSAURS

The second key group of Triassic marine reptiles was the nothosaurs. They appeared in the Early Triassic, as

some time back in the Carboniferous; their long history during the Permian is as yet unrepresented by fossils. This idea now seems rather unlikely. It is more probable that ichthyosaurs are derived diapsids, that evolved from some terrestrial form possibly similar to Youngina (page 50) during the Late Permian. It must be stressed, however, that this proposal is very recent, and the evidence is far from overwhelming: but there simply does not seem to be any other alternative.

The oldest known ichthyosaurs, *Utatsusaurus* and *Grippia*, have long-snouted skulls and streamlined bodies. The well-formed paddles show no indication of the

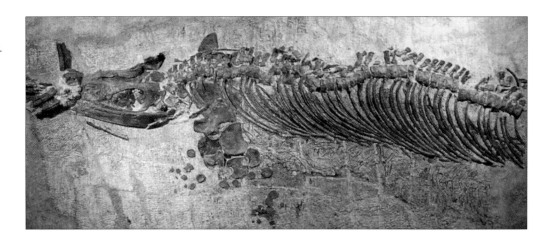

The Mid Triassic ichthyosaur Cymbospondylus, *and the nothosaur* Ceresiosaurus *(below). Both specimens come from the renowned marine beds of Monte San Giorgio, Switzerland.*

did the ichthyosaurs, but died out before the end of the period. Nothosaur fossils are best known from the Middle Triassic rocks of central Europe, although the group occurred worldwide in ancient, shallow-marine regions. The excellent record of nothosaur specimens from Germany, Switzerland, and northern Italy is the result of the exceptional preservation conditions noted above for *Mixosaurus*.

Pachypleurosaurus is a typical nothosaur, which shows the remarkable range in size even within a single species, or between species of one genus: from eight inches to 13 feet (one-fifth to four metres) in this case. The neck and tail are long, the head is small, and the limbs are paddle-like. *Pachypleurosaurus* was mainly aquatic in adaptations, using wide sweeps of its deep tail to produce swimming thrust. The paddles may have been used to some extent in steering, but they were probably held along the sides of the body most of the time, in order to reduce drag. The shoulder girdle and

hip girdle are relatively small and only weakly attached to the vertebral column, so that they could not have supported the weight of the body on land for long.

The long, lightly built skull has very large eye orbits and nostrils, but small temporal fenestrae. The teeth are pointed cones, rather like those of the ichthyosaurs, and they project sideways and forward. They suggest that *Pachypleurosaurus* fed on small, fast-moving fishes such as paleonisciforms and "holosteans," which the agile nothosaurs could have chased and snapped up with darts of their long necks.

Recently, an embryo nothosaur has been reported from the Middle Triassic of Switzerland. This tiny skeleton, at two inches (five centimetres), is about one-sixth the length of an adult, and it suggests that the nothosaurs may have laid eggs, presumably on land. The specimen shows typical juvenile characters seen in all young vertebrates, including human babies.

For example, the head is relatively large, making up

nearly 25% of the total length, while in adults the figure is about nine per cent. The limb bones are not fully ossified (formed from bone itself), but are still partly in the form of cartilage. In addition, many of the skull bones, such as the frontals, are separate and unfused, while in adults they have fused together completely.

The nothosaurs arose from an as yet unidentified source in the Late Permian or Early Triassic. As with the ichthyosaurs, many ideas have been put forward about their origins; the consensus now seems to be that, like the former, they are also diapsid derivatives, having arisen possibly from an animal broadly similar to *Youngina*. The nothosaurs diversified in the Middle Triassic and dwindled in importance toward the end of the Triassic. A new group, similar to the nothosaurs in many respects – the plesiosaurs – appeared at the end of the Triassic and rose to prominence in the Jurassic and Cretaceous.

UNUSUAL MARINE DIAPSIDS OF THE MIDDLE TRIASSIC

While the ichthyosaurs and nothosaurs were relatively widespread and long-lasting groups, one or two rarer marine forms are known, particularly from the superb Middle Triassic marine mudstones of Switzerland. *Askeptosaurus* was a broadly lizard-like animal, with a long thin body, deep propulsive tail, and moderately long jaws. The feet were large and possibly webbed in life, but otherwise are just like the feet of terrestrial diapsids. The askeptosaurs are known from only one or two genera, and they did not survive the Triassic.

Rather more ridiculous in appearance, and arguably the most unusual reptile of all time, was *Tanystropheus*. Its remains come from the Middle Triassic of Switzerland and adjoining areas. *Tanystropheus* had an incredibly long neck, indeed more than twice the length of its body, as well as a moderately long tail. The neck was not greatly flexible, however, since it is composed of only some nine to 12 cervical vertebrae, each like a long tube. These vertebrae all bear long, thin cervical ribs that run back beneath the spine and may have provided attachments for powerful neck muscles. The function of this neck has been a great mystery – until recent studies of the evolution of the group, and the way in which the neck grew during the lifetime of an individual *Tanystropheus*.

It seems that *Tanystropheus* is a diapsid, of the pro-

The most remarkable fossil of a marine reptile found recently, an embryo nothosaur, Neusticosaurus peyeri, *from Monte San Giorgio. The head is relatively large, and the eye and brain even more so – just as in a human baby. The rather short backbone curves around in a C-shape below the head. In addition to these embryonic proportions, this specimen is demonstrably a juvenile since the limb bones are tiny and not yet fully ossified.*

lacertiform group, related to other Late Permian and Triassic animals that probably looked rather like large lizards. The prolacertiforms are closely related to the archosaurs (page 71), and they are all characterised by rather long necks, but *Tanystropheus* represents rather an extreme of this tendency!

Juvenile *Tanystropheus* had relatively much shorter necks than adults, indeed on a par with the neck length of the more sensible-looking prolacertiforms. As the juveniles became larger, during normal growth, the neck sprouted forward at an accelerated rate. This is another example of the kinds of differences in relative growth rates seen during animal development, and noted above for the baby nothosaur. A modern analogue of *Tanystropheus* might be the giraffe. Baby giraffes have slightly lengthy necks, but not nearly as stretched, in proportion to their body size, as the neck of the adult. During normal growth, the giraffe's neck increases in size at a greater rate than the growth in the rest of its body. If the giraffe's long neck is an adaptation for feeding on leaves from the tops of trees, what was the function of the cervical extravaganza of *Tanystropheus*?

The juvenile *Tanystropheus* had small multi-pointed teeth and seems to have been fully a terrestrial animal that fed on insects and worms. The adult had single-pointed teeth, more like those of standard flesh-eating

reptiles, and it probably ate fish. The limbs may have been used as paddles, and since the skeletons are found in marine sediments, so a largely aquatic adult existence is likely. This sort of habitat and dietary shift from the juvenile to the adult stage is not an unusual phenomenon. Adult *Tanystropheus* are generally reconstructed as coastal swimmers that fed on small fish, caught either by fishing from rocks or by darting the head around underwater.

THE FIRST SHELL-CRUSHERS

Malacivory, the mastication of molluscs (shellfish), is a highly specialised trade that was carried out before the Triassic by some sharks, and after it by some lungfish, crocodilians, and walruses. The placodonts ('armoured teeth') may have been the world's most successful malacivores of all time, but they were restricted to the Middle and Late Triassic. Only ten genera, mainly from central Europe, achieved a remarkable diversity of forms, although all share a number of strange features.

Placodus looks at first like a heavily-built land animal, but its remains are found in coastal marine sediments and it must have been able to swim, even if in a rather lumbering way. It did not use its tail much in swimming, as most other marine reptiles did, since it is not deep enough; and neither are the limbs modified as paddles.

An adult specimen of Neusticosaurus *(above), and the aquatic diapsid* Askeptosaurus *(left).*

However, the limb girdles seem to be too weak to support the weight for long periods of walking and running on land. The massive undercarriage of gastralia, or abdominal ribs, covering the belly is a peculiar placodont feature.

Placodus has a heavily built triangular skull, with large eye orbits placed on top rather than at the sides, and thick reinforced bony struts around the palate. The teeth are the key to placodont success. There are six spoon-like incisor teeth projecting at the front of the mouth, and 14 broad, flattened, black enamel-coated teeth in the roof of the mouth. These are matched by six or eight similar teeth in the lower jaw. The spatulate teeth at the front of the mouth were presumably used

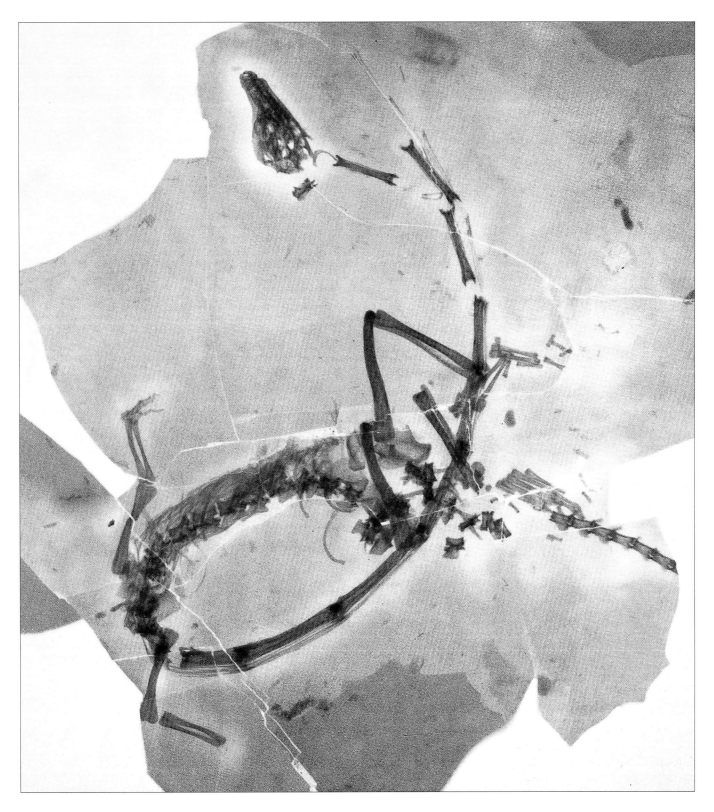

An X-ray photograph of the enigmatic diapsid reptile Tanystropheus, from the Mid Triassic marine mudstones of Monte San Giorgio, Switzerland – the source of so many well preserved fish and reptiles. The head lies at the top, and the nine rod-like vertebrae of the bizarre neck curve right down the picture to the bottom left-hand corner. Each cervical vertebra is a rigid rod, up to one foot (30 centimetres) long, and the whole neck was longer than the rest of the body. The slim trunk curves around as if in a knot, and the tail ends on the right. The slender limbs stretch out on each side of the body, with one hind limb complete and the knee pointing upward and crossing over the neck.

The skeleton of Macrocnemus, *a very close relative of Tanystropheus. It had a long neck, as shown here, but not quite as long as in the latter! The skeleton is flattened, but essentially complete, even including the delicate cervical ribs, which controlled the movements of the neck and its muscles.*

TANYSTROPHEUS

The prolacertiforms, such as Tanystropheus and Macrocnemus, were once thought to be true lizards, but they appear to have closer affinities to the archosaurs. There were several species of Tanystropheus, all with long necks, and the neck length seems to have increased through evolutionary time. The neck contained only nine vertebrae, so it was not as flexible as it might at first seem. It is most likely that Tanystropheus used the neck to dart after the quick-moving fish which formed the bulk of its diet.

for levering molluscs off the rocks in shallow coastal seas, and the shells were cracked between the broad crushing teeth behind. The flesh was extracted and swallowed and the hard, calcareous shell fragments ejected from the mouth. Biomechanical analyses of the unusual placodont skull have shown that the maximum biting force was exerted just in the middle of the palate, where all the crushing teeth lay, and that the jaw-closing adductor muscles ran largely horizontally. On contraction, these muscles closed the jaws firmly and pulled them backward, thus providing the maximum grinding force possible.

Some placodonts have very broad skulls, reminiscent of the rhynchosaurs (page 69), and there was probably a similar reason – namely the great size of the adductor muscles. Some also developed great carapaces of bony

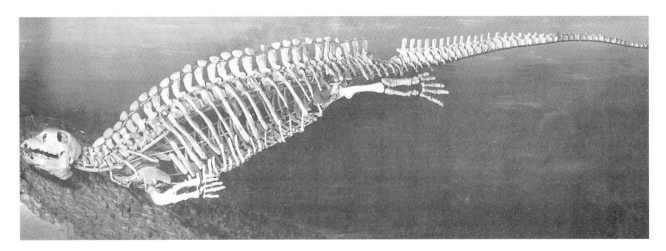

The complete mounted skeleton of Placodus gigas *a typical placodont from the Mid Triassic of southwestern Germany. The body is heavily built, and the placodonts probably swam gracefully, like seals today, although they were probably rather awkward on land. The teeth and jaws are adapted for eating shellfish.*

PLACODUS

The placodonts swam by using their limbs as paddles, rather than by undulating their bodies as in fishes and many other swimming reptiles. Placodus *has a heavy body and a narrow tail, neither of which suits it for fish-like swimming. There are two types of teeth: spade-like incisors at the front, for snipping and scraping oysters from the rocks; and broad circular back teeth that acted as a pounding board to crush the shells, before the flesh was swallowed.*

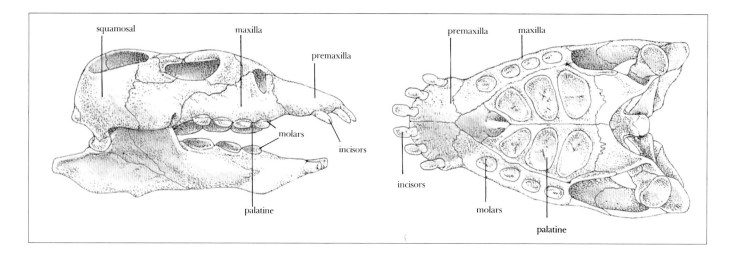

plates which covered the whole body region like the shell of a turtle. The purpose of this armour is rather mysterious, since the placodonts were seemingly large enough, at up to seven feet (two metres) in length, to escape predation by nothosaurs, tanystropheids, and most ichthyosaurs.

Placodont relationships are as uncertain as those of the ichthyosaurs and nothosaurs, and for similar reasons. They are probably diapsid derivatives, but there are no intermediate forms that indicate their ancestry. The placodonts may have arisen from an independent diapsid ancestor in the Late Permian or Early Triassic or, according to a recent analysis, they may share an ancestor with the nothosaurs.

CEPHALOPODS AND FISHES OF THE JURASSIC AND CRETACEOUS

Most of the marine reptiles of the Triassic – the nothosaurs, askeptosaurs, tanystropheids, placodonts, and early ichthyosaurs – did not survive into the Jurassic. There were two mass extinction events in the seas, corresponding to those on land which marked the end of the rhynchosaurs, thecodontians, and most mammal-like reptiles (page 135). These events also marked a new age of cephalopods and fishes.

The nautilus-like ammonoids of the Triassic disappeared, and they were replaced by a major derived group, the ammonites. Ammonites are well-known fossils in nearly all marine rocks of the Jurassic and Cretaceous, not least because they evolved rapidly and exhibit a succession of different forms that give invaluable evidence for the dating of the rocks. Ammonites belong to the large mollusc group, the cephalopods,

The skull of Placodus seen from below (palatal view, right) and from the side (lateral view, left). The bony jaws and palate bear some 20 teeth: six projecting, shovel-like incisors on the premaxillae; four circular, crushing molars on each maxilla; and a further three broad, rectangular molars on each palatine bone. The lower jaw is deeper than the skull itself, indicating that Placodus had massive jaw adductor muscles. These ran from inside the squamosal and parietal bones and the side wall of the brain case, to the outer surface of the lower jaw. On contraction, they powerfully clamped the jaws shut.

which today includes the squid, cuttlefish, octopus, and chambered nautilus. They had coiled shells, often looking like small spiral tractor wheels, and the animal lived in a chamber within the outer whorls of the shell. Close relatives that also lived in the Jurassic and Cretaceous seas were the belemnites. They looked more like squid, with an internal skeleton shaped rather like a bullet, equivalent to the cuttlefish bone. Both of these cephalopod groups provided a major new food source for the marine reptiles.

The fish also evolved into many new forms in the Jurassic and Cretaceous. The hybodont sharks survived from the time of the Triassic, but the modern shark and ray groups, the neoselachians, began to diversify. They show considerable advances over the earlier chondrichthyans in their jaws and swimming abilities. Today's forms have a mobile set of jawbones and a mouth placed beneath the snout, which is very efficient at gouging out large chunks of flesh from the sides of fish and swimming tetrapods (including human beings).

The bony fishes showed a parallel evolutionary radiation. In the Jurassic, the paleonisciforms and holosteans dwindled in importance, although one or two genera of both broad groups survive to the present day. A new group, the teleosts, appeared then and has since proved spectacularly successful, representing today some

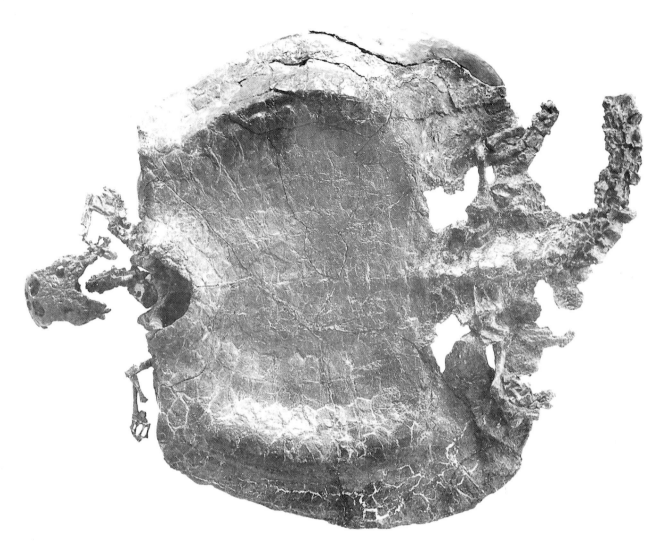

The placodont Henodus chelyops, *an animal that was startlingly similar in body form to the turtles. The origin of the armour is a mystery.*

20,000 species of fish, from sticklebacks to tuna, salmon to anglerfish, and seahorse to haddock. Teleosts appear to owe their success to the fully symmetrical tail fin and the highly mobile, protrusible mouth. When they feed, they open the jaws and telescope them forward rapidly, which creates a suction effect. This can pull in small particles of food and other prey animals alike, depending upon the size of the teleost.

The teleosts of the Jurassic and Cretaceous were diverse in size, form, and habits, including small herring-like fishes, as well as some massive ones like *Xiphactinus*, 17 feet (five metres) long with heavy jawbones and needle-like teeth. One large *Xiphactinus*, from the Late Cretaceous of Kansas, has been found with a fish more than five feet (160 centimeters) long

inside its stomach, and smaller relatives have been reported with as many as 10 recognisable fish skeletons preserved inside them. Teleost fishes were abundant in Jurassic, and especially Cretaceous, seas; like ammonites and belemnites, they provided a rich source of food for reptilian predators, and allowed those predators to radiate widely.

ICHTHYOSAURS OF THE JURASSIC AND CRETACEOUS

The ichthyosaurs continued to evolve after the extinctions of earlier forms in the Late Triassic. The Early Jurassic representatives were little different, and they are known in large numbers from marine beds of that age in Europe and other parts of the world. Indeed, the Early Jurassic ichthyosaurs from the coastal beds of southern England, and Dorset in particular, were some of the first marine reptiles to be found as fossils. Mary Anning, the famous early collector, turned up several superb and complete specimens between 1812 and 1847 (page 10). Similar beautifully preserved ichthyosaur skeletons were found at that time in limestone quarries in southwestern Germany, and both areas continue to produce new material.

Jurassic and Cretaceous ichthyosaurs range in length from three to 53 feet (one to 16 meters), and they retain the dolphin-like body, long snout, large eyes, and limb paddles of the Triassic forms. Some of the Early Jurassic specimens from Germany are preserved as perfectly as those from the Middle Triassic. The limestone quarries around Holzmaden, near Stuttgart, are especially well known for the exquisite detail of their specimens. These quarries have produced hundreds of complete skeletons of young and old ichthyosaurs which show the skeletons in near-perfect articulation (the bones are linked together), and in some cases a black "ghost" of the skin outline. This shows the paddles were extended by skin and connective tissue, the tail fin was roughly symmet-

rical (even though the backbone bends down into its lower part), and there was a high dorsal fin, just as in *Mixosaurus* (page 113).

The Early Jurassic ichthyosaurs of England and Germany show other biological features. Dozens of the German specimens have been analysed for their stomach contents, which show that the diet consisted mainly of squid: the tiny hooklets from their tentacles are found within the ichthyosaur rib cages. They also ate smaller quantities of fish, as shown by the presence of scales in the rib cages; but seemingly no ammonites or belemnites, unless they discarded their shells before swallowing. These ichthyosaurs range in size from 10 to 53 feet (three to 16 metres), and the three or four species that co-existed seem to have fed on different size groups of squid and fish. Interestingly, the coprolites (faecal masses) of ichthyosaurs contain abundant fish bones and scales, but few squid hooks, so it is hard to quantify the diet precisely.

The post-Triassic ichthyosaurs fall into three main groups, distinguished by features of the skull and pad-

dles. They were most abundant in the Early Jurassic, but a few groups lived on into the Late Jurassic, and one into the Mid Cretaceous.

EXPERT SWIMMING REPTILES

Ichthyosaurs appear to have been highly efficient swimmers, showing as they did the highest degree of aquatic adaptation of all the marine reptiles. They swam by beating their deep tails from side to side, and used their front paddles to change direction and to control roll and pitch, just as fishes do. There are no signs at all that they were able to venture onto land: their limbs are entirely modified into paddles, their shape is fish-like, and the limb girdles are so weak that they could not have supported the body weight out of water. Modern marine turtles and crocodilians creep onto land, at least to lay their eggs, and so probably did the extinct plesiosaurs. How did the ichthyosaurs reproduce if they could not do this?

There is remarkable and direct evidence that the ichthyosaurs gave birth to live young in the water, just as whales and dolphins do today. Beautifully preserved skeletons from the Early Jurassic of Germany show two or three embryos within the rib cages of some specimens, and one or two actually show the young in the process of being born, tail first. The effort of giving birth, or some complication during parturition, must have killed both mother and offspring in these cases. Reptiles typically lay eggs, so the ichthyosaurs must have suppressed this stage at an early point in their adaptation to life in the sea. Some modern lizards and snakes do the same thing, but for different reasons, retaining the egg inside the ovary, where the juvenile hatches internally before it is born.

The Early Jurassic Leptopterygius *was preserved in an unusual position, lying in a kind of three-quarters view (right). A close relative was* Stenopterygius *(below). This female has three embryos in the belly area and one being born, tail-first, as in modern dolphins.*

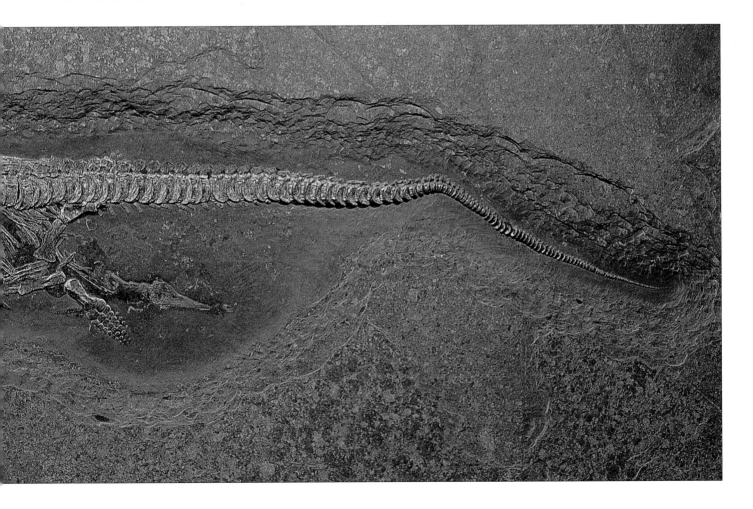

The skull of the Early Jurassic ichthyosaur Leptopterygius *(right), preserved in three dimensions. Note the large sclerotic plates, like a pineapple ring in the eye socket, that supported the huge eyeball.*

The bones of an ichthyosaur in situ from the Late Jurassic of northern France (below). The remains often look rather scrappy in the field, until they have been cleaned up. Many of the fine ichthyosaurs shown in other photographs started off looking like this!

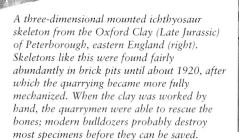

A three-dimensional mounted ichthyosaur skeleton from the Oxford Clay (Late Jurassic) of Peterborough, eastern England (right). Skeletons like this were found fairly abundantly in brick pits until about 1920, after which the quarrying became more fully mechanized. When the clay was worked by hand, the quarrymen were able to rescue the bones; modern bulldozers probably destroy most specimens before they can be saved.

MARINE CROCODILIANS

Crocodilians today are a relatively minor tetrapod group (page 76), but they include one or two marine forms. In the Jurassic, there were rather more marine forms, and some were highly successful. The teleosaurs and geosaurs (metriorhynchids) of the Jurassic and Early Cretaceous are characterised by very long snouts, a large rectangular skull 'window' called the upper temporal fenestra, and short forelimbs.

Geosaurus, from the late Jurassic of Europe, is probably the most marine of these crocodilians. At 10 feet (three metres) long, it was extensively adapted for swimming by lateral fish-like undulations. The vertebrae of the tail bend down, as in ichthyosaurs, to support the tail fin; the limbs are broad and paddle-like; and the normal bony body armor has been lost – a likely aid to streamlining. The geosaurs would have had difficulty in walking on land, although they probably still returned there to lay eggs.

Some long-snouted crocodilians continued to terrorise the oceans after the extinction of the teleosaurs and geosaurs, but none of the later groups ever achieved the former high levels of adaptation. Modern-style crocodilians arose during the Late Cretaceous, but they became more adapted to life on land and the margins of fresh waters.

PLESIOSAURS AND PLIOSAURS

The ichthyosaurs declined somewhat after the Early Jurassic, and the marine crocodilians after the Late Jurassic, and it seems that many of their roles were taken over by the plesiosaurs. The first plesiosaur remains are from the Late Triassic, and it is likely that

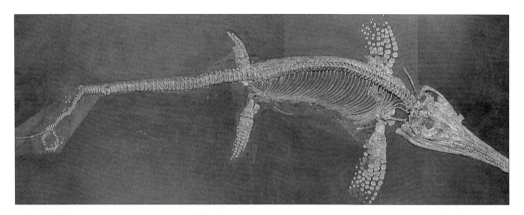

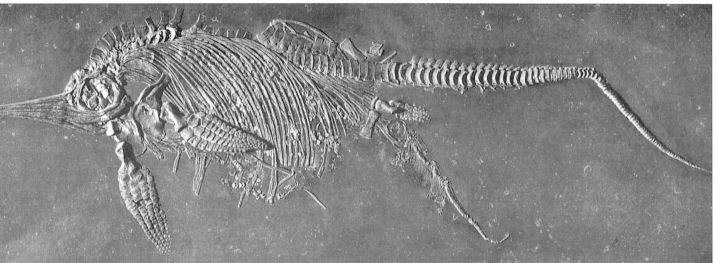

The rib cage of Stenopterygius *(left), showing a complete embryo of about one foot (30 centimeters) in length. The tiny spool-like vertebrae can be seen here, and also within the rib cage area of the other example (above). Ichthyosaurs had to give birth to active young, since they were unable to go onto land to lay eggs.*

Top: An Early Jurassic ichthyosaur from southwestern Germany, showing nearly perfect preservation of a complete skeleton. The disk-shaped vertebrae have toppled over slightly in the tail, like a row of falling circular dominoes.

they arose from the nothosaurs (pages 114–115), but their pattern of evolution is still not completely understood.

The plesiosaurs and pliosaurs were generally larger than the nothosaurs, with body lengths ranging from seven to 47 feet (two to 14 metres). They had well-evolved paddles, rather like those of the ichthyosaurs, and heavily reinforced limb girdles. The plesiosaurs

seem to have followed three or four main lines of evolution, some having long flexible necks and small skulls, and others having shorter necks and massive skulls.

The long-necked plesiosaurids such as *Plesiosaurus*, and the cryptocleidids such as *Cryptocleidus*, have over 30 cervical (neck) vertebrae, a skull with a long snout, and nostrils set well back from the tip of the snout. The teeth are long and conical, and they interlock when the jaws are closed – a typical adaptation of most fish-eaters. The jaw joint is set below the level of the tooth row, which shifts the strongest biting point forward to the front of the jaws, exactly where it is needed for snatching the quick-moving bony fish.

continued on page 128

MARINE REPTILES OF THE LATE JURASSIC

Late Jurassic seas teemed with a diversity of marine reptiles, as shown in this scene based on fossils from England and Germany. The most common forms in many localities were the dolphin-shaped ichthyosaurs, such as *Ichthyosaurus*, which may have hunted in packs and pursued fish, belemnites, and ammonites. Some crocodilians also became highly adapted to life in the sea, a good example being the geosaur *Metriorhynchus* (top right).

A third major marine reptile group were the plesiosaurs, such as *Cryptocleidus* (bottom right), which hunted the common holostean and teleost fishes. The giant pliosaurs, such as *Liopleurodon* (middle and left), were also members of the plesiosaur group. They hunted small prey such as ammonites, as shown here, but they could no doubt have fed on all of the other marine reptiles.

How the world looked in this period

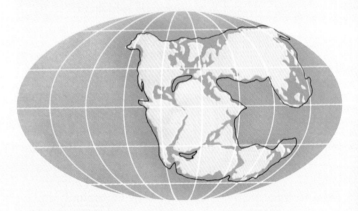

One of the marine giants of all time was the pliosaur Liopleurodon (1), at almost 40 feet (12 metres) in length. The other marine reptiles shown were of similar size to each other: the ichthyosaur Ichthyosaurus (2), the crocodilian Metriorhynchus (3), and the plesiosau Cryptocleidus (4).

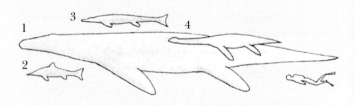

The third line of evolution included elasmosaurs of the Cretaceous, such as *Muraenosaurus*, which took the long-necked adaptations to an extreme. Some had as many as 70 cervical vertebrae, and the neck could bend around upon itself two or three times. The elasmosaurs no doubt jabbed their snake-like necks rapidly among the scattering schools of teleost fishes. They could have darted the head in and out and seized several fish without moving the body at all.

An early find of an *elasmosaur* skeleton, *Elasmosaurus*, in the US in 1868, may have sparked one of the most remarkable feuds that palaeontology has ever seen. The specimen was described by Edwin Cope, who mistakenly placed the tiny skull at the end of the tail instead of in its correct position. His contemporary, Othniel Marsh, was quick to point out the mistake. The skull was rapidly transferred to the other end of the skeleton, but the damage had been done. It is said that Cope never forgave Marsh for his public humiliation, and Marsh sought to find fault with Cope thereafter. The two palaeontologists competed with each other for the remainder of their lives.

The fourth plesiosaur lineage, represented by the pliosauroids, evolved in the opposite direction. They lost cervical vertebrae, the number reducing from 30 in early pliosauroids to 13 in later ones, and the skull grew larger. *Kronosaurus*, a pliosaur from the Late Cretaceous of Australia, was up to 40 feet (12 metres) long, and its skull formed one-fifth of that length. The pliosauroids were clearly top predators which fed on smaller - plesiosaurs, ichthyosaurs, crocodilians, and turtles, as well as large fish and ammonities.

Plesiosaur movement has been a subject of intensive research and controversy in recent years. The trunk was surprisingly rigid, so that plesiosaurs could not have thrown their bodies into sinuous waves in order to produce swimming thrust. Both the shoulder and pelvic girdles were long, heavily built, sledge-like structures, and they were linked by a firm belly armour of broad

Marine crocodilians: Metriorhynchus from the Late Jurassic (above), and Steneosaurus from the Early Jurassic (right), both from Germany. The skull shape is superficially similar, although they had different origins. The posterior portion is square, and the long, extremely narrow snout is lined with curved, sharp needle-like teeth, used for trapping and holding fish. These crocodilians had light armour, and swam by beating their tails from side to side

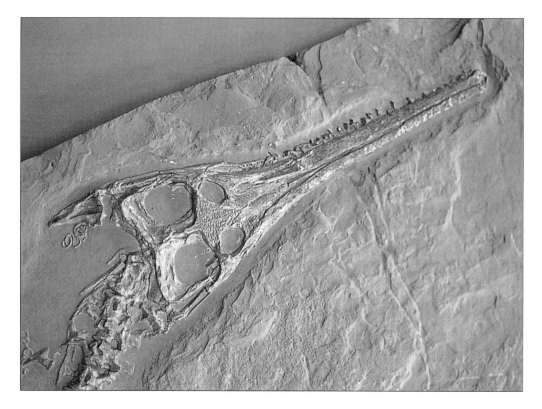

Digging up plesiosaurs (above): a typical site for marine reptiles of the Late Jurassic – Dogsthorpe brick pit, near Peterborough, eastern England. Hand searching of these sites by geologists turns up many bones and occasional complete skeletons. An old reconstructed scene, representing the marine reptiles – about this time (below), now turns out to be rather romanticised. Nevertheless, climates were probably warmer than today, and primitive mammals roamed the land.

MARINE TURTLES

Turtles and tortoises share a common body plan in which the skeleton is fused inside a two-part 'shell', with the carapace above and the plastron below. The 'shell' is made from bone and covered by horn, and it is the horn that may give the colour: many tortoises, in particular, show astounding colour patterns. The shell is an integral part of the skeleton, probably derived from outgrowths of the ribs; it is not possible for a turtle to slip out of its shell if it becomes too hot, despite many cartoons to that effect!

The turtles appeared in the Late Triassic. They were mainly a terrestrial group until the Late Jurassic, when one or two moderate-sized specimens have been found in coastal marine sediments. These animals may have fed on small fish or slow-moving invertebrates in s hallow waters.

The first fully marine turtles seem to be the protostegids, such as *Archelon*, known best from the Late Cretaceous of North America. *Archelon* was a 13-foot (four-metre) giant with a hooked, toothless jaw and broad, paddle-like feet. Its carapace and plastron were composed of broad star-shaped plates that did not form a complete bony covering over the body. This was doubtless a weight-saving device in order to assist swim-

continued on page 133

abdominal ribs. The whole formed a single, inflexible, reinforced body unit. Similarly, the tail was probably of little use in generating thrust, since it was usually small. As a result, palaeontologists have focused on the use of the paddles in swimming. Three main models have been proposed: rowing, flying, and modified flying (pages 130–131).

SWIMMING IN THE SEA

The marine reptiles of the Mesozoic era were highly successful animals, and they competed for food with large bony fish and sharks. Their swimming abilities must have been as good as those of the fish, and there has been much debate recently about exactly how the various reptiles propelled themselves through the water.

Ichthyosaurs look so much like sharks and other fish in their body shape, that it has always been assumed they swam in the same way. Doubtless, the body was thrown into lateral undulations, and the tail was swept from side to side, thus producing a forward thrust. The front paddles were used to prevent rolling and yawing of the body, and for steering. The small posterior paddles well may have contributed to stabilisation.

Likewise, the ancient marine turtles are assumed to have used the swimming techniques of their closest living relatives, the modern sea turtles. They have rigid bodies (the carapace and plastron prevent fishy undulations!), and the large front paddles beat in a figure-of-eight to produce a kind of "underwater flying."

Most attention has focused on the swimming mode of the plesiosaurs, creatures which have no obvious modern analogue. Did they swim by rowing, by underwater flying, or by some intermediate motion of the paddles?

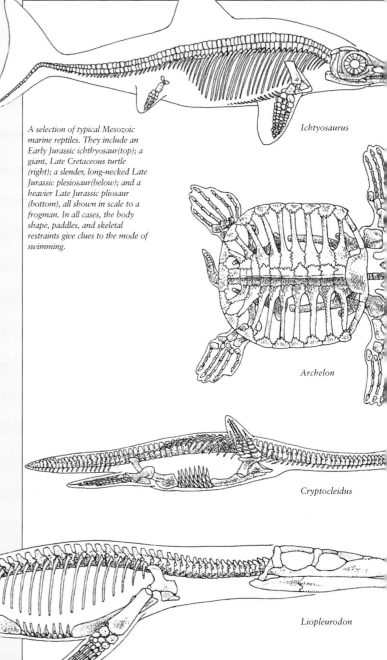

A selection of typical Mesozoic marine reptiles. They include an Early Jurassic ichthyosaur(top); a giant, Late Cretaceous turtle (right); a slender, long-necked Late Jurassic plesiosaur(below); and a heavier Late Jurassic pliosaur (bottom), all shown in scale to a frogman. In all cases, the body shape, paddles, and skeletal restraints give clues to the mode of swimming.

Ichtyosaurus

Archelon

Cryptocleidus

Liopleurodon

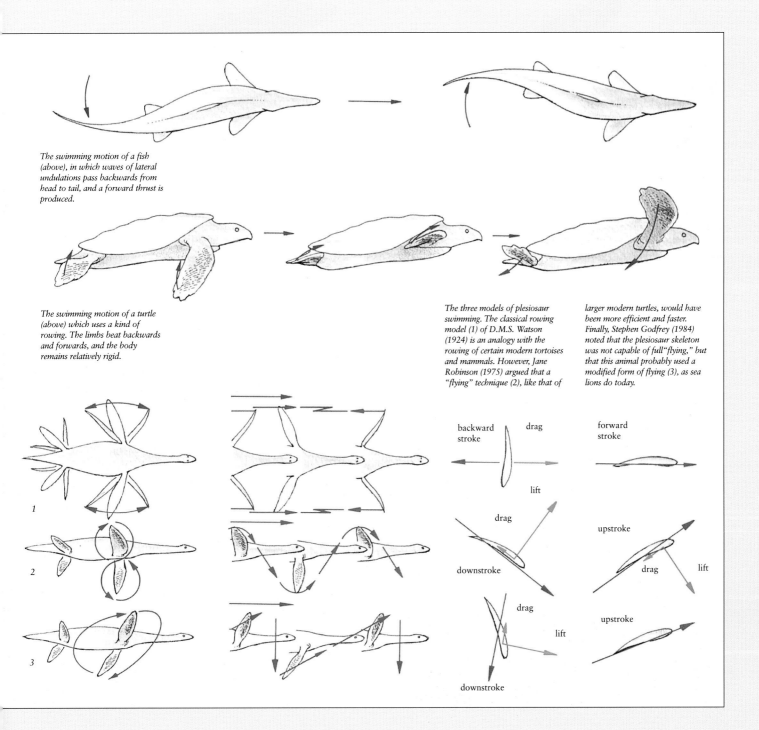

The swimming motion of a fish (above), in which waves of lateral undulations pass backwards from head to tail, and a forward thrust is produced.

The swimming motion of a turtle (above) which uses a kind of rowing. The limbs beat backwards and forwards, and the body remains relatively rigid.

The three models of plesiosaur swimming. The classical rowing model (1) of D.M.S. Watson (1924) is an analogy with the rowing of certain modern tortoises and mammals. However, Jane Robinson (1975) argued that a "flying" technique (2), like that of larger modern turtles, would have been more efficient and faster. Finally, Stephen Godfrey (1984) noted that the plesiosaur skeleton was not capable of full "flying," but that this animal probably used a modified form of flying (3), as sea lions do today.

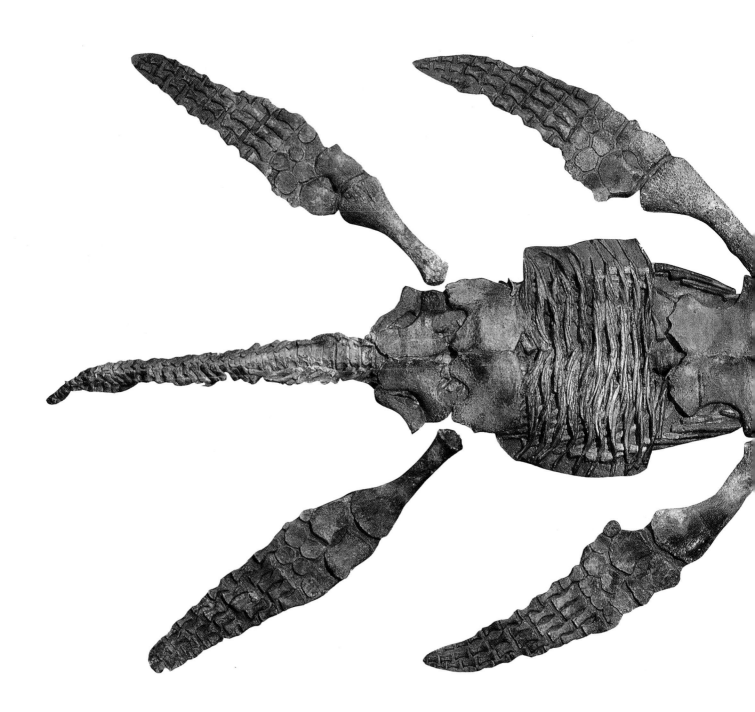

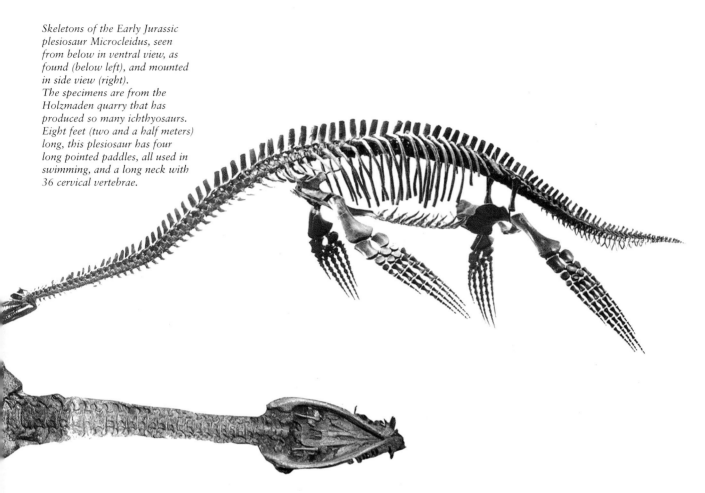

Skeletons of the Early Jurassic plesiosaur Microcleidus, seen from below in ventral view, as found (below left), and mounted in side view (right). The specimens are from the Holzmaden quarry that has produced so many ichthyosaurs. Eight feet (two and a half meters) long, this plesiosaur has four long pointed paddles, all used in swimming, and a long neck with 36 cervical vertebrae.

ing. The protostegids, unlike the usual image of sluggish land-living turtles, were effective and rapid swimmers that probably fed on large fish.

The protostegids disappeared by the end of the Cretaceous, but new marine lineages evolved after that. Today there are several successful large-sized marine turtles, that spend most of their time in the surface waters of the oceans, and only return to land to lay their eggs. They are often large – the leatherback has a shell length of nearly seven feet (two metres), and weighs 1,000 pounds (500 kilograms).

MOSASAURS, THE GIANT MARINE LIZARDS

The first mosasaur to be discovered was historically a very important fossil that figured in post-revolutionary wars in late eighteenth-century Europe. The mosasaurs are only one of three families of anguimorph lizards that became adapted to life in the sea during the Late Cretaceous, but they are the most spectacular. Today, the anguimorphs include the monitor lizards and the limbless anguids, which are very different from the

mosasaurs which ranged up to 33 feet (10 metres) in length!

There were some 20 genera of mosasaurs, abundant in certain chalk seas in the Late Cretaceous of Europe and midwestern North America. *Plotosaurus*, a typical North American form, has a long body, deep tail, and paddle-like limbs. In each finger and toe, the number of phalanges (individual bones of the digits) is greater than in their closest relatives, the monitor lizards; this is a feature of other marine reptiles, too.

The heavy jaws are lined with sharp conical teeth that may have been used for capturing fish, and were certainly used for cracking open ammonites. This has been demonstrated by the discovery of ammonite shells that bear rows of regular puncture marks – which precisely match the spacing, size, and pattern of mosasaur teeth. One ammonite shell shows clearly how a young mosasaur snatched the living cephalopod and bit it once, but without crushing the shell. The reptile then opened its jaws, rotated the shell and bit again, before giving up and swimming off in search of easier prey. The mosasaur jaw is characterised by the presence of an

A Late Jurassic pliosaur (right) from the English Oxford Clay. The long powerful skull was adapted for grappling with other marine reptiles, as well as with large fish. The paddles are extremely large, in order to provide powerful enough propulsion when chasing the smaller ichthyosaurs and plesiosaurs that formed its diet.

PLOTOSAURUS

extra joint in the middle, which probably increased the gape and biting force.

The mosasaurs seem to have moved into ecological niches vacated by the ichthyosaurs, crocodilians, and plesiosaurs in the Late Cretaceous. Yet they too died

A moderate-sized mosasaur, Plotosaurus does not look very much like a varanid (monitor) lizard, and yet the skull and skeleton show abundant evidence of their close relationship. Plotosaurus was so modified to a successful life in the sea that it was probably unable to venture onto land. Swimming propulsion was produced by lateral undulations of the body and tail, and steering was carried out by the paddles.

out, along with the dinosaurs, at the end of the period. Why did so many important reptile groups die out at that time?

THE GREAT EXTINCTION

The reign of the reptiles ended 65 million years ago, at the great extinction event of the Cretaceous-Tertiary time boundary. This is often abbreviated to the K-T event (K is the contraction for Cretaceous, from the Greek *kreta*, meaning chalk). Reptiles lived on to the present day, of course – crocodilians, lizards, snakes, and turtles – but they have been eclipsed by the birds and mammals. What happened 65 million years ago to mark the end of so many spectacular reptiles on land, in the air, and in the seas?

The first task, in trying to answer this question, is to establish the exact pattern of the extinction: what died out and what survived? And what was the timing of the extinctions? The major reptile groups that disappeared were the dinosaurs on land, the pterosaurs in the air, and the plesiosaurs and mosasaurs in the sea. The marine crocodilians and ichthyosaurs had died out long before the end of the Cretaceous and so should not be included in the list. Other vertebrates became extinct at the same time: several families of birds and marsupial mammals, and a few families of teleost fishes.

In addition to this extinction, a variety of important invertebrate groups disappeared in the sea: the ammonites, belemnites, and other molluscs, and a num-

The skull of Mosasaurus maximus *from the Navesink Formation (Late Cretaceous) in New Jersey. The structure of the skull allows great flexibility, just as in its much smaller relatives, the living lizards. Indeed, there were several joints in the skull, and even in the middle of the lower jaw, that would have allowed Mosasaurus to open its mouth in a vast gape in order to swallow large prey. It seems remarkable, in view of the tremendous modification of the mosasaurs to marine life, that the group was relatively short-lived.*

ber of families of planktonic organisms.

The survivors of the K-T event include the majority of fish, amphibians, turtles, lizards, snakes, and placental mammals, which show no unusual fluctuations in numbers at the time. Of course, one or two families of each of these large groups disappeared within five million years either side of the K-T event, but that is a typical level of "background" extinction – the normal turnover that takes place throughout the history of any group.

Among other organisms, most invertebrates seem to have been little affected. For example, there is no detectable increase from the background extinction rate for gastropods, most bivalves, corals, crustaceans (crabs), insects, and others. There is also little long-term interruption to the evolution of land plants.

It is not easy to establish any measure of selectivity between the groups that died out and those that survived. Certainly, most of the marine extinctions were among swimmers rather than bottom-dwellers. On land, the spectacular extinctions at least were among groups of larger animals. However, there are so many exceptions to these rules that they do not carry a great deal of weight; the extinctions seem to have been ran-

dom in their effects.

THE TIMING OF THE EXTINCTIONS

It is probably harder to study the timing of the K-T event than to establish what went extinct. The problems relate to correlation and dating.

Correlation, in geological terms, is the matching of rocks from certain parts of the world with others deposited at the same time. In order to determine whether the K-T event happened rapidly and at exactly the same time worldwide, an independent means of correlating rocks deposited on land and in the sea is needed. Since correlation on a global scale depends to a large extent on comparison of fossil faunas, there is a problem of developing a circular argument. In other words, it is assumed that the K-T boundary lies just above the last occurrence of dinosaur bones in a geological section, and this level can be identified and correlated worldwide. However, can we be sure that the dinosaurs died out at the same time everywhere? If not, then the boundary does not correspond to a single instant in geological time, and it can only confuse our attempts to assess the timing of events.

An independent technique of correlation may be developed from magnetostratigraphy. This is the study of magnetic reversals in the history of the Earth. At irregular intervals, and for uncertain reasons, the magnetization of the north and south poles of the Earth flips over. The direction of the field is preserved by the

The skull of a mosasaur, Prognathodon solvayi, *from the Late Cretaceous chalk of Belgium. The skull is very loosely built, as in modern lizard relatives, and the extra joint in the middle of the lower jaw is particularly evident. The teeth are adapted for puncture-crushing; that is, piercing shells or tough-skinned prey and crushing in order to extract the flesh. The partial ring of bony plates in the eye, the sclerotic plates, supported the eyeball. These are typical of reptiles that hunted under water and used their large eyes to see in the murky conditions.*

orientation of magnetised iron-rich grains in the rocks being deposited at the time. These directions can be recorded from sand-stones deposited in ancient deserts, rivers, and seas, and they can be correlated fairly precisely. Studies are currently being made and may offer stronger evidence in the future. However they also indicate dating problems, which must be solved.

Dating of the Earth's rocks is possible because certain of them contain unstable, naturally radioactive materials. Over time, these break down at a steady rate. It is possible to backtrack from the present degree of breakdown in such rocks, to estimate the exact age of their formation in terms of millions of years. Good as the technique is, it is still subject to a variety of errors, and it cannot yet achieve levels of accuracy that would allow ages to be measured in terms of thousands of years – which would help enormously around the time of the K-T event. Indeed, there is often a margin of error of several million years. Such inaccuracy is not helpful to scientists trying to study a biological crisis like the K-T event.

Nevertheless, it seems that many fossil groups did not

The great age of the reptiles: a rather imaginative scene in the Late Cretaceous, as envisaged by an artist in a popular science text of 1885. Two rather awkward-looking pterosaurs squawk in the sky, over a shallow sea which contains a vaguely crocodile-like ichthyosaur, and a plesiosaur with a snaking neck and a surprised expression. A number of turtles creep about on the shore beneath the tropical vegetation. Some faintly dove-like birds in the sky near the top left complete the scene.

die out exactly at the K-T time boundary. Rather, they show patterns of decline over ten million years or more before that boundary. For example, the diversity of belemnites, ammonites, plesiosaurs, pterosaurs, and dinosaurs declined step by step over the final part of the Cretaceous period, until there was only a handful of species of each group immediately before the end.

GRADUALISM AND CATASTROPHISM

The two main current theories for the K-T extinctions are the gradualist and the catastrophist models, although each has numerous variants. In a nutshell, the gradualist model is that the extinctions lasted over ten million years or so, and that they were caused by gradual changes in climate (possibly a cooling and increase in seasonality) and in sea-water conditions. The evidence for the gradualist scenario comes mainly from studies of the decline of various animal groups, and geological evidence for changes in climate and sea level.

The catastrophist model is that the extinctions occurred essentially overnight, after the Earth was hit by an asteroid seven miles (10 kilometers) in diameter. The impact buried the asteroid deep within the crust and sent an enormous explosive cloud of rock fragments and dust into the atmosphere. The dust remained in the upper atmosphere, where it was swept around the globe and blocked out the Sun for half a year. This pre-

vented photosynthesis and growth in land plants and plant plankton, and hence led to catastrophic extinctions due to lack of food. There is geochemical evidence for one or more extraterrestrial impacts on the Earth at the K-T boundary, and the physical model of the dust cloud is plausible.

There are problems with both models. The gradualist scenario does not explain why so many groups that had been in decline, suddenly seemed to give up the ghost just at the same time. On the other hand, the catastrophic models have been rather unsuccessful at explaining exactly how organisms were killed, and why most were not. Also the impact, or impacts, can only have caused parts of the extinction, since so many groups had already been in decline – presumably for other reasons – for many millions of years.

At present, there is no obvious resolution to the problem, despite the attentions of scores of geologists, palaeontologists, geochemists, and astrophysicists, and the publication of hundreds of research reports every year.

Nevertheless, the K-T event marks the end of the reign of the reptiles. They had been hugely successful on Earth for 220 million years or more. They occupied every continent, they conquered every lifestyle on land, in the air, and in the sea. They showed as much diversity as do the mammals today. The living reptiles may seem a poor and motley legacy from those great times of the late Paleozoic and Mesozoic eras, but of course the reptiles rule on today – rather, the feathered reptiles and hairy reptiles. It is only an arbitrary human decision that drew the line and separated the birds and mammals from the reptiles.

NAMES OF FOSSIL AMPHIBIANS AND REPTILES

Fossil animals such as amphibians and reptiles are given scientific names when they are first made known to the scientific world. The names are sometimes self-explanatory, but more often they seem to be rather obscure, and frequently unpronounceable!

This guide to the names of the animals mentioned in this book gives details of the pronunciation and meaning of the name. The names have usually been derived from Greek or Latin terms that may say something about the creature or the means of its discovery. Finally, the scientists who described each animal for the first time, and named it, are given together with the date.

Acanthostega
ay-KANTH-o-STEE-ga
Horn-spine
E. Jarvik 1952

Anurognathus
ah-NEW-rog-NATH-us
Tailless jaw
L. Dîderlein 1923

Archaeopteryx
AR-kee-OP-ter-ix
Ancient wing
R. Owen 1864

Archelon
ar-KEE-lon
Ancient turtle
G. R. Wieland 1896

Askeptosaurus
a-SKEPT-o-SAW-rus
Unthoughtful reptile
F. Nopcsa 1925

Campylognathoides
KAMP-ile-og-NATH-oi-deez
Curved jaw
K. Strand 1928

Capitosaurus
CAP-it-o-SAW-rus
Head reptile
G. MÅnster 1836

Captorhinus
KAP-tor-INE-us
Deceptive snout
E. D. Cope 1895

Cheirotherium
KIRE-o-THEE-ree-um
Hand beast
J. J. Kaup 1835

Coelurosauravus
SEEL-oo-ro-SAWR-a-vus
Hollow-tail reptile
R. L. Carroll 1978

Cotylorhynchus
kot-ILE-or-INK-us
Cup snout
J. W. Stovall 1937

Crassigyrinus
CRASS-ih-JY-rin-us
Thick frog
D. M. S. Watson 1929

Cryptocleidus
KRIP-toe-KLIDE-us
Hidden closed-tooth
H. G. Seeley 1892

Ctenochasma
TEEN-oh-KAS-ma
Comb gape
H. von Meyer 1852

Dendrerpeton
DEN-drer-PEAT-on
Tree reptile
R. Owen 1853

Dicynodon
dy-SY-no-don
Two dog-tooth
R. Owen 1845

Diictodon
dy-IK-to-don
Two-blow tooth
R. Broom 1913

Dimetrodon
dy-MET-ro-don
Two long-tooth
E. D. Cope 1878

Dimorphodon
dy-MORF-o-don
Two-form tooth
R. Owen 1859

Dinodontosaurus
DY-no-DON-to-SAW-rus
Terrible-tooth reptile
A. S. Romer 1943

Diplocaulus
DI-plo-KAW-lus
Two-fold stem
E. D. Cope 1877

Dorygnathus
DORE-eeg-NATH-us
Spear jaw
A. Wagner 1860

Edaphosaurus
eh-DAF-o-SAW-rus
Earth reptile
E. D. Cope 1883

Elasmosaurus
eh-LAZ-mo-SAW-rus
Plate reptile
E. D. Cope 1868

Endothiodon
EN-do-THY-o-don
Within-sulfur reptile le
R. Owen 1876

Eogyrinus
EE-oh-jih-RINE-us
Early frog
D. M. S. Watson 1926

Eryops
ER-ee-ops
Draw face
E. D. Cope 1887

Erythrosuchus
er-ITH-ro-SOOK-us
Red reptile
R. Broom 1905

Eudimorphodon
YOO-dy-MORF-oh-don
True two-form tooth
R. Wild 1978

Euparkeria
YOO-park-EE-ree-a
True Parker's
R. Broom 1913

Geosaurus
GEE-oh-SAW-rus
Earth reptile
G. Cuvier 1842

Germanodactylus
jer-MAN-oh-DAK-tih-lus
German finger
C. C. Young 1964

Gnathosaurus
NATH-oh-SAW-rus
Jaw reptile
H. von Meyer 1834

Grippia
GRIP-ee-a
For Dr. Gripp
C. Wiman 1928

Henodus
HEN-oh-dus
One tooth
F. von Huene 1936

Hovasaurus
HOVE-a-SAW-rus
Hova (Madagascar) reptile
J. Piveteau 1926

Hylonomus
HY-lo-NOME-us
Wood law
W. Dawson 1860

Hyperodapedon
HY-per-oh-DAP-eh-don
Upper pavement-tooth
T. H. Huxley 1859

Icarosaurus
IK-ah-roe-SAW-rus
Icarus reptile
E. H. Colbert 1966

Ichthyosaurus
IK-thee-oh-SAW-rus
Fish reptile
W. Koenig 1818

Ichthyostega
IK-thee-oh-STEEG-a
Fish spine
G. SÑve-Sîderbergh 1932

Ictidosuchops
IK-tid-oh-SOOK-ops
Blow crocodile face
A. W. Crompton 1955

Kannemeyeria
KAN-eh-MAY-er-ee-a
For Mr. Kannemeyer
H. G. Seeley 1909

Kayentatherium
ka-YEN-ta-THEE-ree-um
Kayenta beast
H. D. Sues 1983

Kingoria
king-OH-ree-a
For Mr. King
C. B. Cox 1959

Kronosaurus
KRONE-oh-SAW-rus
Kronos (Greek god) reptile
H. A. Longman 1930

Kuehneosaurus
KYOO-nee-oh-SAW-rus
Kuehne's beast
P. L. Robinson 1957

Leptopleuron
LEP-toe-PLOO-ron
Slender rib
R. Owen 1851

Leptopterygius
LEP-toe-TER-ij-ee-us
Slender wing
F. von Huene 1922

Lesothosuchus
less-OH-toe-SOOK-us
Lesotho crocodile
K. N. Whetstone and
P. J. Whybrow 1983

Liopleurodon
LY-oh-PLOO-ro-don
Smooth-sided tooth
H.E. Sauvage 1873

Longisquama
LONG-ih-SQUAM-a
Long scale
G. Sharov 1970

Lycaenops
ly-KINE-ops
Wolf face
R. Broom 1925

Lystrosaurus
LISS-tro-SAW-rus
Spoon reptile
E. D. Cope 1870

Macrocnemus
MAK-ro-NEEM-us
Long leg
F. Nopcsa 1931

Massetognathus
mass-ET-og-NAY-thus
Chewer jaw
A. S. Romer 1967

Megazostrodon
MEG-a-ZOS-tro-don
Big-girdle tooth
A. W. Crompton and
F. R. Jenkins 1968

Mesosaurus
MEEZ-o-SAW-rus
Middle reptile
P. Gervais 1869

Metriorhynchus
MET-ree-oh-RINK-us
Measure reptile
H. von Meyer 1830

Microcleidus
MIKE-ro-KLIDE-us
Small closed-tooth
D. M. S. Watson 1911

Mixosaurus
MIX-oh-SAW-rus
Mixed reptile
G. Baur 1887

Morganucodon
MOR-gan-OOK-oh-don
Morgan's tooth
W. G. Kåhne 1949

Mosasaurus
MOZE-a-SAW-rus
Meuse reptile
W. D. Conybeare 1822

Moschops
MOS-chops
Calf eye
R. Broom 1911

Muraenosaurus
MOO-rine-oh-SAW-rus
Moray eel reptile
H. G. Seeley 1874

Neusticosaurus
NEW-stik-oh-SAW-rus
Swimming reptile
H. G. Seeley 1882

Ophiacodon
OAF-ee-AK-o-don
Snake tooth

O. C. Marsh 1878

Ornithocheirus
OR-nith-oh-KIRE-us
Bird hand
H. G. Seeley 1869

Ornithosuchus
OR-nith-oh-SOOK-us
Bird crocodile
E. T. Newton 1893

Oudenodon
oo-DEN-oh-don
Nothing tooth
R. Owen 1860

Pachypleurosaurus
PAK-ee-PLOO-ro-SAW-rus
Thick-rib reptile
F. Broili 1927

Paleothyris
PAL-ee-oh-THY-ris
Ancient door
R. L. Carroll 1969

Parasuchus
PAR-a-SOOK-us
Near crocodile
T. H. Huxley 1870

Petrolacosaurus
PET-rol-AK-oh-SAW-rus
Oil rock reptile
P. D. Lane 1945

Placodus
PLAK-oh-dus
Plate tooth
L. Agassiz 1833

Plagiosuchus
PLAJ-ee-oh-SOOK-us
Crosswise crocodile
F. von Huene 1922

Planocephalosaurus
PLAN-oh-KEF-al-oh-SAW-rus
Flathead reptile
N. C. Fraser 1983

Plesiosaurus
PLEEZ-ee-oh-SAW-rus
Ribbon reptile
W. D. Conybeare 1821

Plotosaurus
PLOT-oh-SAW-rus
Swimmer reptile
C. L. Camp 1951

Podopteryx
PODE-op-TER-ix
Foot-wing
G. Sharov 1970

Probelesodon
PRO-bel-ez-OH-don
Before fine-tooth
A. S. Romer 1962

Procolophon
pro-KOL-oh-FON
Before summit
R. Owen 1876

Procynosuchus
pro-SINE-oh-SOOK-us
Before dog-crocodile

R. Broom 1937

Prognathodon
prog-NATH-oh-don
Before jaw-tooth
L. Dollo 1889

Proterogyrinus
PRO-ter-oh-JY-rin-us
Earlier frog
A. S. Romer 1970

Proterosuchus
PRO-ter-oh-SOOK-us
Earlier crocodile
R. Broom 1903

Pteranodon
ter-AN-oh-don
Wing toothless
O. C. Marsh 1876

Pterodactylus
TER-oh-DAK-ty-lus
Wing-finger
G. Cuvier 1809

Pterodaustro
TER-oh-DOW-stro
Southern wing
J. F. Bonaparte 1970

Quetzalcoatlus
KWET-zal-KO-at-lus
Quetzalcoatl (Aztec god)
D. A. Lawson 1975

Rauisuchus
ROW-ih-SOOK-us
Gray crocodile
F. von Huene 1942

Rhamphorphynchus
RAM-for-INK-us
Curving snout
H. von Meyer 1847

Rhynchosaurus
RINK-oh-SAW-rus
Snout reptile
R. Owen 1842

Saurosuchus
SAW-ro-SOOK-us
Reptile crocodile
O. A. Reig 1959

Scaphonyx
SKAF-on-ix
Boat claw
A. S. Woodward 1907

Scutosaurus
SKOOT-oh-SAW-rus
Armor reptile
A. Hartmann-Weinberg
1930

Serpianosaurus
SER-pee-AN-oh-SAW-rus
Creeping reptile
O. Rieppel 1989

Shunosaurus
SHOO-no-SAW-rus
Shu (Sichuan) reptile
Z. Dong, S. Zhow and
Y. Chang 1983

Sordes
SOR-dayz
Devil
G. Sharov 1971

Stagonolepis
STAG-on-oh-LEP-is
Spine scale
L. Agassiz 1844

Staurikosaurus
STOR-ik-oh-SAW-rus
Cross reptile
E. H. Colbert 1970

Steneosaurus
STEN-ee-oh-SAW-rus
Narrow reptile
E. Geoffrey Saint-Hilaire
1825

Stenopterygius
STEN-oh-TER-ij-ee-us
Narrow wing
O. Jaekel 1904

Tanystropheus
TAN-ee-STROFF-ee-us
Long twisted
H. von Meyer 1852

Tapinocephalus
TAP-in-oh-KEF-al-us
Low head
R. Owen 1876

Terrestrisuchus
ter-EST-ri-SOOK-us
Earth crocodile
P. J. Crush 1984

Thrinaxodon
thrin-AX-oh-don
Trident tooth
H. G. Seeley 1894

Youngina
yung-INE-a
For Mr. Young
R. Broom 1914

MUSEUMS

Nearly all general museums around the world, and especially natural history museums, have some specimens of fossil reptiles on show. They may be examples found locally, since fossil reptiles are known from all parts of the world, or they may be specimens or casts from elsewhere. The continuing popularity of fossil reptiles with museum visitors means that new examples are displayed all the time. Larger museums often feature special shows of dinosaurs and other fossil reptiles.

The list of museums includes the major ones in each country, with their specialist reptile collections. But it cannot be complete since over 10,000 museums world-wide have some fossil reptiles on display! There are also many major temporary exhibits which cannot be covered here.

AFRICA

Bernard Price Institute of Palaeontology
Johannesburg, South Africa.
Permian, Triassic and
Jurassic mammal-like
reptiles and crocodilians.

Musée National du Niger
Niamey, Niger.
Saharan Cretaceous marine
and terrestrial reptiles.

Museum of Earth Sciences
Rabat, Morocco.
Jurassic terrestrial reptiles.

National Museum of Zimbabwe
Harare, Zimbabwe.
Early Jurassic crocodilians.

South African Museum
Cape Town, South Africa.
Permian and Triassic
mammal-like reptiles, early
mammals, crocodilians.

ASIA

Geology Museum
Indian Statistical Institute,
Calcutta, India.
Mesozoic reptiles from India.

Institute of Vertebrate Paleontology and Paleoanthropology
Peking, China.
Large collection of Chinese
Permian and Mesozoic
reptiles.

Mongolian Academy of Sciences
Ulan Bator, Mongolia.
Late Cretaceous mammals
and lizards.

Museum of Natural History
Osaka, Japan.
Mesozoic marine reptiles.

National Science Museum
Tokyo.
Various Japanese fossils,
especially marine reptiles.

AUSTRALIA

Australian Museum
Sydney, New South Wales.
Australian fossil reptiles.

Queensland Museum
Fortitude Valley,
Queensland.
Australian Mesozoic fossil
reptiles.

EUROPE

Bayerische Staatssammlung fär Geologie und historische Geologie
Munich, West Germany.
Jurassic marine reptiles,
pterosaurs, and
Archaeopteryx.

Bristol City Museum
Bristol, England.
Jurassic marine reptiles.

Central Geological and Prospecting Museum
Leningrad
Mesozoic reptiles from
Russia and Mongolia.

Elgin Museum
Elgin, Scotland.
Triassic reptiles.

Institut und Museum fur Geologie und Palaontologie
Tubingen, Germany.
Marine reptiles, pterosaurs.

Institut of Paleobiology
Warsaw, Poland.
Mammals and lizards from
the Early Cretaceous of
Mongolia.

Institut Royal des Sciences
Naturelles
Brussels, Belgium.
Early Cretaceous
crocodilians.
Leicestershire Museum
Leicester, England.
Jurassic marine reptiles.
Museum of Isle of Wight Geology
Sandown, England.
Early Cretaceous turtles,
crocodilians.
Museum National d'Histoire
Naturelle
Paris, France.
Fossil reptiles from France,
North Africa, and elsewhere.
Natural History Museum
London, England.
Jurassic marine reptiles and oth-
ers.
Naturhistorisches Museum
Berlin, East Germany.
East African pterosaurs,
German Permian and Triassic
reptiles.
Palaeontological Institute
Moscow,
Fossil reptiles from all parts of
the former Soviet Union.
Palaontologisches Museum
Zurich, Switzerland.
Triassic marine reptiles.
Sedgwick Museum of Geology
Cambridge, England.
British Mesozoic and Tertiary
reptiles.
Senckenberg Museum
Frankfurt, West Germany.
Jurassic marine reptiles and
pterosaurs, Tertiary reptiles.
Stuttgart Naturhistorisches
Museum
Stuttgart, West Germany.
German Triassic and Jurassic
reptiles.
University Museum
Oxford, England.
Jurassic marine reptiles.

NORTH AMERICA
Academy of Natural Sciences
Philadelphia, Pennsylvania.
North American marine reptiles
and others.
American Museum of Natural
History
New York, New York.
Large collection of Permian and
Mesozoic reptiles.
Carnegie Museum of Natural
History
Pittsburgh, Pennsylvania.
North American fossil reptiles
from the West.
Denver Museum of Natural
History
Denver, Colorado.
Jurassic and Cretaceous reptiles.
Earth Sciences Museum
Provo, Utah.
Jurassic fossil reptiles of the West.
Field Museum of Natural History
Chicago, Illinois.
Permian and Mesozoic reptiles
from North America.
Los Angeles County Museum
Los Angeles, California.
Various western fossil reptiles.
Museum of Comparative
Zoology
Cambridge, Massachusetts.
Carboniferous, Permian, and
Mesozoic reptiles from North
and South America.
Museum of Northern Arizona
Flagstaff, Arizona.
Triassic reptiles.
Museum of Paleontology
Berkeley, California.
Triassic and Jurassic reptiles from
the western United States.
Museum of the Rockies
Bozeman, Montana.
Late Cretaceous reptiles.
National Museum of Natural
History
Washington, D.C.
Carboniferous, Permian,
Mesozoic, and Tertiary reptiles
from North America.
National Museum of Natural
Sciences
Ottawa, Ontario.
Canadian fossil reptiles.
Peabody Museum of Natural
History
New Haven, Connecticut.
Jurassic and Cretaceous reptiles.
Redpath Museum
Montreal, Quebec.
Carboniferous and Permian rep-
tiles.

Royal Ontario Museum
Toronto, Ontario.
Canadian fossil reptiles.
Tyrrell Museum of Paleontology
Drumheller, Alberta.
Late Cretaceous fossil reptiles.
University of Wyoming
Geological Museum
Laramie, Wyoming.
Jurassic and Cretaceous terrestrial
and marine reptiles.
Utah Museum of Natural History
Salt Lake City, Utah.
Late Jurassic reptiles.

SOUTH AND CENTRAL
AMERICA
Museo Argentino de Ciencias
Naturales
Buenos Aires, Argentina.
Mesozoic terrestrial reptiles.
Museum of La Plata University
La Plata, Argentina.
South American Mesozoic rep-
tiles.
Museu Nacional
Rio de Janiero, Brazil.
Triassic and Jurassic reptiles.
Natural History Museum
Mexico City, Mexico.
Mesozoic and Tertiary reptiles.

INDEX

CREDITS

Quarto would like to thank the following for their help in compiling this book. Every effort has been made to obtain copyright clearance, and we do apologize if any omissions have been made. **p6** Ann Ronan; **p7** (above) Dr Jennifer Clack, (below) Ann Ronan; p8 Geoscience Features Picture Library; **p9** (left) British Museum (Natural History), (right) AnnRonan; **p10** Dr R Wild; p11 British Museum (Natural History); **p14** NASA; **p15** Anglo Australian Telescope Board; **p16** National Museums of Scotland; **p17** Dr S Conway Morris; **p20** Dr S Conway Morris; **p21** Dr S Conway Morris; **p23** (left) Science Photo Library, (right) Dr S M Andrews; **p27** (top left) Dr E Buffetaut, (top right) Dr Jennifer Clack, (bottom left) Dr Jennifer Clack; **p30** Science Photo Library; **p31** (above) Dr R Wild, (below) Dr R Wild; **p32** Dr R Wild; **p34** Dr Donald Baird; **p35** (left) McGill University (right) Mr G Gauld; **p38** Dr Donald Baird; **p39** Dr Michael Benton; **p40** Dr Donald Baird; **p43** Field Museum of Natural History Chicago; **p46** Dr Donald Baird; **p49** Dr Michael Benton; **p52** (top left) Dr Donald Baird, (below) Dr C Gow; **p53** Dr C Gow; **p54** Dr C Gow; **p55** (above) Dr Gillian King, (middle) Dr Gillian King, (below) Dr C Gow; **p65** (left) Dr Gillian King, (right) Dr C Gow; **p57** Dr A R I Cruickshank; **p58** (above) Dr Michael Benton, (below) Dr Gillian King; **p61** Dr S E Evans; **p62** Dr Michael Benton; **p63** Dr A R I Cruickshank; **p64** (above) Dr Donald Baird, (below) Dr Gillian King; **p66** (top left) Dr Donald Baird (top right) Dr A R I Cruickshank; **p68** Dr Michael Benton; **p69** Dr Michael Benton; **p70** Dr Michael Benton; **p71** Dr A R I Cruickshank; **p75** Dr R Wild; **p76** Dr Gillian King; **p83** Science Photo Library; **p84** Dr Donald Baird; **p86** Dr Michael Benton; **p87** Dr Michael Benton; **p88** Dr R Wild; **p91** (above) Dr R Wild, (below) Dr Michael Benton; **p94** Dr R Wild; **p95** Dr R Wild; **p101** Dr P Wellnhofer; **p104** Dr P Wellnhofer; **p108** Ann Ronan; **p109** Professor H Rieber; **p112** Dr Michael Benton; **p113** Professor H Rieber; **p114** (above) Dr M Sander, (below) Professor H Rieber **p115** Dr M Sander; **p116** (above) Dr M Sander, (below) Dr Michael Benton; **p117** Professor H Rieber; **p118** Professor H Rieber; **p119** Dr F Westphal; **p121** Dr F Westphal; **p122/3** Dr R Wild; **p124** (left) Dr R Wild, (middle) Dr Michael Benton, (right) Dr M A Taylor; **p125** (above) Dr R Wild; (middle), Dr R Wild (below) Dr R Wild; **p128** (above left) Dr A R I Cruickshank, (below right) Dr E Buffetaut; **p129** (above) Dr M A Taylor, (below) Ann Ronan; **p132** Dr R Wild; **p133** Dr R Wild; **p134** Dr Michael Benton; **p135** Dr Donald Baird; **p136** Mr T Lingham-Soliar; **p137** Ann Ronan. Dinosaur reconstructions: Graham Rosewarne; skeletal diagrams Jim Robins; charts and diagrams: Janos Marffy, Sally Launder.